German
for
Singers

German for Singers

A TEXTBOOK OF DICTION AND PHONETICS

William Odom
University of Southern Mississippi

SCHIRMER BOOKS
A Division of Macmillan Publishing Co., Inc.
NEW YORK

Collier Macmillan Publishers
LONDON

Schirmer Books
A Division of Macmillan Publishing Co., Inc.
866 Third Avenue, New York, N. Y. 10022

Collier Macmillan Canada, Ltd.

Library of Congress Catalog Card Number: 80-5493

Printed in the United States of America

printing number

2 3 4 5 6 7 8 9 10

Library of Congress Cataloging in Publication Data

Odom, William (William McBride)
  German for singers.

  Includes index.
  1. Singing—Diction. 2. German language—Pronunciation. I. Title.
MT883.035   784.9'32   80-5493
ISBN 0-02-871750-3   AACR2

Tape recordings of all exercises and song texts contained in this book are available. For further information, contact the author.

To
Roy Harris Odom

A genius quite,
He's a wonderful wight.

Smith and de Koven
Act I, Robin Hood

Contents

Alphabetical Index

Spelling	Pronunciation	Position	Example	Page
a	[ɑ]	all positions	Amerika [ɑˈmeɾIkɑ]	87
aa	[ɑ]	all positions	Saal [zɑl] hall	87
ai	[ɑe]	all positions	Mai [mɑe] May	105
au	[ɑo]	all positions	Haus [hɑos] house	105
ay	[ɑe]	all positions	Bayer [ˈbɑeɒ] Bavarian	105
ä*	[ɛ]	all positions	Händel [ˈhɛndəl]	90
äu	[ɔø]	all positions	Häuser [ˈhɔøzɒ] houses	108
b	[b]	1. before vowel, *l,* or *r* in one element	Eber [ˈebɒ] boar geblickt [gəˈblIkt] glimpsed	75
		2. before *l, n,* or *r* in derivatives or inflected forms	ebne [ˈebnə] level	
	[p]	1. final 2. preconsonantal 3. final in element	Grab [grɑp] grave liebst [lipst] (you) love Halbinsel [ˈhɑlpˌʔInzəl] peninsula abreisen [ˈɑpˌɾɑezən] depart	75
bb	[b]	in one element	Ebbe [ˈɛbə] ebb	75
	[pb]	in two elements	abbauen [ˈɑpˌbɑoən] dismantle	75
c	[ts]	before a front vowel	Citrone [tsiˈʦɾonə] lemon	137
	[k]	before a back vowel	Café [kɑˈfe] cafe	137
ch	[χ]	after back vowels	Bach [bɑχ] brook	30, 137
	[ç]	after front vowels and consonants	ich [Iç] I Mädchen [ˈmɛtçən] girl	30, 137
	[k]	in some words of Greek origin	Orchester [ɔɾˈkɛstɒ] orchestra	138
chs	[ks]	in one element	sechs [zɛks] six	142
	varied	in two elements	see Chapter 15	142

* The vowel *ä* is sometimes spelled *ae;* the pronunciation remains the same.

Spelling	Pronunciation	Position	Example	Page
ck	[k]	in all positions	nicken ['nIkən] nod	131
d	[d]	1. before vowel or *r* in one element	Ader ['adɒ] artery bedrohen [bə'droən] threaten	78
		2. before *l, n,* or *r* in derivatives or inflected forms	edler ['edlɒ] noble	
	[t]	1. final	Freund [frɔønt] friend	78
		2. preconsonantal	widmen ['vItmən] dedicate	
		3. final in element	fremdartig ['frɛmt͵ʔartIç] strange	
dd	[d]	in one element	Widder ['vIdɒ] ram	78
	[td]	in two elements	Raddampfer ['rat͵dampfɒ] paddle steamer	78
dt	[t]	in one element	Städte ['ʃtɛtə] cities	79
	[tt]	in two elements	Handtuch ['hant͵tuχ] towel	
e	[e]	1. before *h*	geht [get] goes	44
		2. doubled	Beet [bet] (flower-)bed	
		3. before C	beten [betən] pray	
		4. before CC in some words	Erde ['erdə] earth stets [ʃtets] always	
	[ɛ]	1. before CC	Bett [bɛt] bed	45
		2. before C in a few words	des [dɛs] of the weg [vɛk] away	
		3. in the prefixes er-, her-, ver-, zer-	erfahren [ɛɒ'farən] experience	
	[ə]	1. final unaccented	Liebe ['libə] love	47
		2. medial unaccented	liebevoll ['libəfɔl] loving	
		3. unaccented prefixes and endings	beginnen [bə'gInən] begin meines ['maenəs] of my	
ei	[ae]	in one element	mein [maen] my	105
eu	[ɔø]	in one element	Leute ['lɔøtə] people	108
ey	[ae]	in all positions	Meyer ['maeɒ]	105
f	[f]	in all positions	fein [faen] fine	148
ff	[f]	in one element	treffen ['trɛfən] meet	148
	[ff]	in two elements	auffahren ['aof͵farən] rise	148
g	[g]	1. before vowel, *l,* or *r* in one element	Geld [gɛlt] money Glück [glYk] happiness	82
		2. before *l, n,* or *r* in derivatives or inflected forms	eigner ['aegnɒ] own	

C = Single consonant; CC = two or more consonants.

Spelling	Pronunciation	Position	Example	Page
	[k]	1. final	lag [lɑk] was lying	82
		2. preconsonantal	klagt [klɑkt] laments	
		3. final in element	bergab [bɛrk'ʔap] downhill	
		4. in *-ig* before *-lich*	königlich ['kønIklIç] royal	
	[ç]	in *-ig* when final or preconsonantal	heilig ['haelIç] holy	82
			heiligt ['haelIçt] consecrates	
	[ʒ]	in some words of French origin	Genie [ʒe'ni] genius	82
gg	[g]	in one element	Flagge ['flɑgə] flag	83
	[kg]	in two elements	weggehen ['vɛk,geən] go away	83
gn	[gn]	in one element	Gnade ['gnɑdə] mercy	83
h	[h]	initially in a word or element	Hand [hɑnt] hand	121
			woher [vo'heɒ] whence	
	silent	elsewhere after a vowel	Floh [flo] flea	121
			gehen ['geən] go	
i	[i]	1. before h	ihn [in] him	36
		2. before C	mir [miɒ] me	
	[ɪ]	1. before CC	bist [bIst] (you) are	37
		2. in the suffixes *-in, -nis, -ig*	Freundin ['frɔøndIn] (girl) friend	
			Kenntnis ['kɛntnIs] knowledge	
			giftig ['gIftIç] poisonous	
		3. in *-ik* if unaccented	Lyrik ['lyrIk] lyrics	
		4. in some short words before C	mit [mIt] with	
			in [In] in	
ie	[i]	all positions except final in some words	die [di] the	92
			Melodie [melo'di]	
	[jə]	final in some words	Arie ['ɑrjə] aria	92
j	[j]	in most words	ja [jɑ] yes	122
			Major [mɑ'joɾ]	
	[ʒ]	in some words of French origin	Journal [ʒuɾ'nal]	122
k	[k]	in all positions	kaum [kɑom] hardly	131
kk	[k]	in one element	Akkord [ɑ'kɔrt] chord	131
kn	[kn]	in all positions	Knabe ['knɑbə] lad	131
l	[l] (dental, "bright")	in all positions	hell [hɛl] bright	112
ll	[l]	in one element	fülle ['fYlə] fill	112
	[ll]	in two elements	fühllos ['fyllos] unfeeling	112

C = Single consonant; CC = two or more consonants.

Spelling	Pronunciation	Position	Example	Page
m	[m]	in all positions	mein [mɑen] my	150
mm	[m]	in one element	Flamme ['flɑmə] flame	150
	[mm]	in two elements	ummalen ['Um͵mɑlən] repaint	
n	[n]	in all positions	nein [nɑen] no	151
ng	[ŋ]	in one element	Finger ['fIŋɒ]	151
	[ng]	in two elements	hingehen ['hIn͵geən] go there	
nk	[ŋk]	in one element	dunkel ['dUŋkəl] dark	151
	[nk]	in two elements	ankommen ['ɑn͵kɔmən] arrive	
nn	[n]	in one element	Tanne ['tɑnə] fir	151
	[nn]	in two elements	annehmen ['ɑn͵nemən] accept	
o	[o]	1. before *h* 2. doubled 3. before C 4. before CC in some words	ohne ['onə] without Boot [bot] boat schon [ʃon] already gross [gros] great hoch [hoχ] high	53
	[ɔ]	1. before CC 2. before C in a few words	doch [dɔχ] but ob [ɔp] whether von [fɔn] of	55
ö*	[ø]	1. before *h* 2. before C 3. before CC in some words	fröhlich ['frølIç] merry schön [ʃøn] lovely grösser [grøsɒ] greater trösten ['trøstən] console	49
	[œ]	before CC	möchte ['mœçtə] would like	50
p	[p]	in all positions	Pein [pɑen] pain	126
pf	[pf]	in all positions	Pfad [pfɑt] path	127
ph	[f]	in all positions	Phantasie [fɑntɑ'zi]	127
pp	[p]	in one element	Lippe ['lIpə] lip	126
ps	[ps]	in all positions	Psalm [psɑlm]	127
qu	[kv]	in all positions	Quarz [kvɑrts]	134
r	[ɒ]	1. final in some monosyllables 2. in the prefixes *er-, her-, ver-, zer-*	der [deɒ] the mir [miɒ] to me vergessen [fɛɒ'gɛsən] forget	28, 116

C = Single consonant; CC = two or more consonants.
* The vowel *ö* is sometimes spelled *oe;* the pronunciation remains the same.

Spelling	Pronunciation	Position	Example	Page
		3. the suffix *-er*	bitter ['bItɒ]	
	[ɾ]	all other positions	fahren ['faɾən] drive	27, 116
			warten ['vaɾtən] wait	
			Meer [meɾ] sea	
rr	[ɾ]	in one element	sperren ['ʃpɛɾən] lock	27, 116
	[ɒɾ]	usually, in two elements	Vorrede ['foɒˌɾedə] introduction	
s	[z]	1. before a vowel	singen ['zIŋən] sing	95
		2. before *l, n,* or *r* in derivatives or inflected forms	unsre ['Unzɾə] our	
	[s]	1. final	Betrugs [bə'tɾuks] (of) deceit	95
		2. before a consonant	Dresden ['dɾesdən]	
		3. final in element	Lesart ['les,ʔaɾt] version	
		4. before a vowel in some exceptions	Erbse ['ɛɾpsə] pea	
sch	[ʃ]	in one element	Schule ['ʃulə] school rasch [ɾaʃ] quickly	101
	[sç]	in two elements	Röschen ['ɾøsçən] little rose	102
sp	[ʃp]	initial in element	spielen ['ʃpilən] play Glockenspiel ['glɔkənˌʃpil]	99
	[sp]	1. medial or final (one element)	Wespe ['vɛspə] wasp	99
		2. in two elements	Liebespaar ['libəsˌpaɾ] couple ausprägen ['aosˌpɾɛgən] stamp	
ss	[s]	in one element	müssen ['mYsən] must	96
	varied	in two elements	see Chapter 10	96
st	[ʃt]	initial in element	stellen ['ʃtɛlən] place verstellen [fɛɒ'ʃtɛlən] disguise	99
	[st]	1. medial or final (one element)	Laster ['lastɒ] vice ist [Ist] is	99
		2. superlative *-st*	schnellste ['ʃnɛlstə] fastest	
		3. in two elements	austragen ['aosˌtɾagən] carry out	
t	[t]	in all positions	Tal [tal] valley	129
th	[t]	in one element	Theater [te'atɒ]	130
	[th]	in two elements	Rathaus ['ɾathaos] town hall	130

Spelling	Pronunciation	Position	Example	Page
ti	[tsɪ]	in the syllable *-tion*	Nation [nɑ'tsion] nation	130
tsch	[tʃ]	in one element	Deutsch [dɔøtʃ] German	130
tt	[t]	in one element	Fittich ['fɪtɪç] wing	129
	[tt]	in two elements	Bettag ['bet‚tɑk] day of prayer	129
tz	[ts]	in one element	setzen ['zɛtsən] set	123
	[tts]	in two elements	entzücken [ɛnt'tsYkən] delight	123
u	[u]	1. before *h* 2. before C 3. before CC in some words	Ruhe ['ruə] rest Mut [mut] courage Gruss [grus] greeting Buch [buχ] book	58
	[U]	1. before CC 2. before C in a few words	muss [mUs] must um [Um] around zum [tsUm] to the	59
ü*	[y]	1. before *h* 2. before C 3. before CC in some words	fühle ['fylə] feel für [fyɒ] for Wüste ['vystə] desert grüssen ['grysən] greet	40
	[Y]	before CC	fünf [fYnf] five	41
v	[f]	in words of Germanic origin	viel [fil] much	146
	[v]	in most words of foreign origin	Vase ['vazə] vase	147
w	[v]	in all positions	Wein [vɑen] wine	144
x	[ks]	in all positions	Hexe ['hɛksə] witch	134
y	[y]	before C	Lyrik ['lyrIk] lyrics	40
	[Y]	before CC	idyllisch [i'dYlIʃ] idyllic	41
z	[ts]	in all positions	Zeit [tsɑet] time Kreuz [krɔøts] cross	123
zz	[ts]	in words of Italian origin	Skizze ['skItsə] sketch	123

C = Single consonant; CC = two or more consonants.
* The vowel *ü* is sometimes spelled *ue;* the pronunciation remains the same.

Preface

This book has two main objectives: (1) to give the singer a systematic approach to pronouncing any German word; and (2) to provide the singer with a phonetic shorthand for making notations above trouble spots in a score.

A number of features have been introduced to assist the user in achieving these objectives.

International Phonetic Alphabet. The *International Phonetic Alphabet* (IPA) is becoming an increasingly important tool in music diction. A number of foreign-language dictionaries and English dictionaries use IPA symbols to give pronunciations. Most diction manuals present the IPA for passive recognition only, as an aid in checking pronunciation in dictionaries. This text departs from this practice by providing exercises in transcribing into the IPA, as well as exercises in reading transcriptions. The intention is to provide singers with a tool which they can use throughout their careers to make notes on German scores or to help in languages with which they are unfamiliar. Singers always develop their own shorthand anyway, so it is well to guide them to a sure and universally accepted system early in their careers.

This book uses English examples to introduce the IPA. Since English-speaking singers already know the sounds, they can concentrate on learning the symbols. In addition, they should be able to retain the symbols more easily since they can associate them with familiar English words rather than foreign words.

The introduction to German pronunciation is greatly facilitated by knowing the IPA beforehand since most of the sounds of German are transcribed with symbols already mastered in the section on English phonetics. The symbols can thus serve as visual cues to the German sounds from the beginning.

Exceptions. Included in every section on German pronunciation is a list of the exceptions to the rules, with their translations. Unfortunately, there are quite a few of these that occur regularly in vocal literature. The serious student is urged to memorize as many as possible.

Exercises. The pronunciation exercises consist of words which contain the sound or sounds under discussion, including exceptions. If one spelling has more than one pronunciation, words in which the spelling is pronounced differently are mixed randomly in the exercises to assure that the student can recognize the conditions for the different pronunciations. The great majority of the examples have been culled directly from vocal literature, complete with endings and prefixes.

Excerpts. Accompanying each section on German pronunciation are excerpts from vocal literature. In each case an attempt has been made to find excerpts which contain high concentrations of the letter or cluster under discussion and low concentrations of letters not yet treated.

Folk songs. The folk songs, some of which are in fact simplified art songs, provide almost daily practice in singing German. Since they are musically very simple, they enable the student to focus on pronunciation. In most cases, songs have been chosen which have relatively high concentrations of the sounds discussed in the sections immediately preceding them.

Art songs. The art songs in the body of the text and in Appendix B are intended for thorough preparation by the student. In general, they have not been chosen because they illustrate some phonetic point but rather because they are commonly performed by voice students. Since the songs are frequently heard and performed, the student will gain maximum long-range benefit from preparing them thoroughly, perhaps even memorizing them.

German for Singers is designed specifically for use in a three-hour university course. Because of its thorough treatment of phonetics, it can be used as the first in a sequence of diction courses in which a command of phonetics can then be assumed. If, however, training in phonetics is received elsewhere or if a two-hour course is offered, all of Part One and most of the transcription exercises in Part Two can conveniently be eliminated.

I must express my warmest thanks to Vivian Wood, without whose support, advice, and encouragement this book would have never been possible.

German
for
Singers

Part One | Phonetics

Chapter 1 | Introduction to Phonetics

THE IPA

Consider the words *ski, key, quay,, me, meat, meet, siege, seize, people,* and *amoeba.* They all contain the vowel sound traditionally represented in American dictionaries as ē.

Now consider the words *wage, wag, wad, wall, ago,* and *many.* Although the vowel *a* appears in each word, it represents a different sound in each; these sounds have been traditionally indicated as ā, ă, ä, ô, ǝ, and ĕ respectively.

If we now include foreign languages in our discussion, it becomes clear that the sound ē has a number of yet different spellings and that the letter *a* has a number of yet different pronunciations. Although the number of sounds that human beings use in speaking is limited, it is apparent that the variety of spellings for these sounds can be bewildering. To facilitate the business of learning pronunciation it would seem logical to have a system in which one symbol represents one sound. The International Phonetic Association, which was founded in 1886, had as one of its chief objectives to create just such a system. The result was the International Phonetic Alphabet or IPA. Although not the only such alphabet, the IPA has become the most widely accepted one and is used in many of the standard references consulted by singers.

This textbook goes a step further than most diction manuals by giving the singer active practice in transcribing sounds into the IPA. Every singer needs a shorthand for jotting down pronunciations. As often as not, the singer will not copy a transcription directly from a reference book but will note down on a score a pronunciation which is troublesome or a correction given by a teacher or coach. In either event, it is convenient to have a ready command of the IPA in order to note down a pronunciation. Furthermore, if skill is achieved in writing the IPA, then it will be even easier for the singer to read transcriptions.

VARIATIONS IN SOUNDS

The exercises in the following chapters no doubt will generate lively discussions over which symbols to use in certain instances. Two factors must be taken into consideration in trying to resolve such questions.

First, one should consider the range of speech sounds as a continuum, much like the light spectrum. When we think of green, a variety of colors comes to mind. What we consider to be green is actually a somewhat arbitrarily chosen section of wavelengths which fades into yellow on one end and into blue on the other. Likewise, each IPA symbol represents not one sound but a family of closely related sounds. Thus the *t* sound is quite different in *top, stop, pot, rotten,* and *bottle* but will still be represented by [t] in the IPA.[1] Vowels also change their color depending on the nature of the consonants surrounding them. The *e* in *bed* does not have exactly the same sound as the *e* in *bet* or *bell,* but all may be represented by the IPA symbol [ɛ]. So, just as the word *green* can indicate a variety of shades, the symbols [t] or [ɛ] can indicate a range of sounds.

Second, the choice of a symbol for a certain sound is affected by individual pronunciation. Certainly, differences in accent will give rise to differences in pronunciation. But even within the same dialect group there are considerable differences in pronunciation. Individual differences can be well demonstrated with a spectrograph, or voiceprint, which is a printed recording of sound patterns. Although the voiceprint reflects aspects of speech other than pronunciation, it is theorized that a voiceprint, like a fingerprint, is not the same for any two people.

Confusion over the choice of symbols will be minimized if the students strive to represent not so much what they say but what they think the best singers would sing.

---

[1] The IPA has developed diacritic marks to reflect subtleties of difference, but they will not be used in this text.

Chapter 2 | Transcribing Sounds

THE SYMBOLS

Before we begin a discussion of transcription, a few notes on the conventions followed in transcribing are in order.

Sound versus Letter

A *sound* is always represented by an IPA symbol in square brackets: [t]; a *letter* is printed in italics: *t*.

Stress

The main, or primary, stress in a word is indicated by a vertical line above and to the left of the syllable, as in *intend* [In'tɛnd]. The secondary stress heard in some words is indicated with a vertical line below and to the left of the syllable, as in *episode* ['ɛpI,soUd].

Length

In the IPA, *length* refers to the amount of *time* it takes to pronounce a sound, not to the quality of the sound. Thus the vowel in *mad* is actually longer than that in *mate,* although traditionally the sound of *a* in *mate* would be called "long *a*" and indicated as ā. In IPA transcription length is indicated with a colon. The word *bead,* with a longer vowel sound, might appear in transcription as [bi:d] and the word *beat,* with a shorter vowel, as [bit].

This concept of length is of little importance to the singer in English diction and will not be used in transcriptions. The situation in German is discussed in Chapter 6.

Symbols

One of the great advantages of the IPA is that it is based on the English alphabet. Many of the symbols for sounds are identical with the letters which represent the sounds. Thus the sound of the letter *t* is represented by the symbol [t]. The student should note that the following consonant symbols are used to denote the sounds most commonly associated with the letters of the same form: [b, d, f, g, h, k, l, m, n, p, r, s, t, v, w, z].

One Sound: One Symbol

When transcribing, do not be misled by spelling; always assign a symbol for each sound. Often, several letters are used to represent one sound, such as *ough* in *bought*, which is transcribed [bɔt]. Conversely, one letter may be used to represent two or more sounds, such as *x* in *fix*, which is transcribed [fIks].

No punctuation, such as a capital or an apostrophe within a word, is reflected in IPA transcription. Thus *Pete's* is rendered as [pits].

VOWELS

Monophthongs

[i] and [I]

The symbol [i] represents the sound of *i* in *ski*. It represents this sound regardless of how it is spelled. Thus we see that the words listed at the beginning of this section—*ski, key, quay, me, meat, meet, siege, seize, people, amoeba*—would be transcribed [ski, ki, ki, mi, mit, mit, siʒ, siz, pipəl, ə'mibə].

The symbol [I] represents the sound of *i* in *skit*, which would be transcribed as [skIt].

Exercise 2.1   Transcribe the following words:

1. pit, peat, Pete
2. bit, bits, bead, beads
3. nick, Nick, nix, nicks, Nick's
4. deep, dip, dips, dipped
5. be, been, bean, beans
6. fill, fills, filled, field
7. kick, quick, squeak, squeaked
8. sieve, seize, peace, piece, please

[ɛ] and [æ]

The symbol [ɛ] represents the vowel sound in *bed* [bɛd]. The symbol [æ] represents the vowel sound in *cat* (kæt].

Exercise 2.2   Transcribe the following words:

1. bet, bat, fad, fads
2. bread, bred, breed, brad

3. guest, gassed, guessed, geese
4. ten, bend, banned
5. dint, dents, dance, dense
6. Nat's, gnats, nest, knack
7. incentive, indent, deeds, dens

Before the nasal sounds [m] and [n], [ɛ] becomes [I] in some regional accents. Thus the pronunciation of *pen* and *pin* is the same: [pIn]. If in doubt in some cases, consult a dictionary and always bear in mind that emulating the diction of the great singers is a sound approach.

Exercise 2.3

Read the following transcriptions aloud, then write down the words they represent. Some may have more than one spelling.

1. [spIn, splin, tæks, spɛnd, ɛk'spænd]
2. [sInd, sɛnt, bægz, tækt]
3. [dI'kænt, kiz, friz, bær, pær]
4. [rI'list, dI'siv, 'rɛspIt, rI'sInd]
5. [tɛkst, pik, 'æ,spɛkt, 'klæsIk, Im'prɛst]
6. [il, livz, 'dædI, 'frɛndlI, ,ækwI'ɛs]
7. [pæst, kwIn'tɛt, prIs'tin, prInts, 'pærIs]

[ɑ] and [ɔ]

The symbol [ɑ] represents the sound of *a* in *father* ['fɑðər]. The symbol [ɔ] represents the vowel sound in *hall* [hɔl]. As with [I] and [ɛ], there is a certain amount of overlap between [ɑ] and [ɔ], which varies from region to region and even from individual to individual. A norm should be sought with the help of dictionaries and good recordings.

Exercise 2.4

Transcribe the following words:

1. all, awl, fall, pause, paws
2. palm, calm, qualms, hot, pods
3. cot, caught, Don, dawn
4. clawed, clod, naught, not
5. far, for, park, pork
6. wrought, rot, rat, gnawed, nod

[U] and [u]

The symbol [U] represents the vowel sound in *book* [bUk]. The symbol [u] represents the vowel sound in *boot* [but].

Exercise 2.5

Transcribe the following words:

1. nook, put, full, fool
2. moons, prove, route, foot
3. look, Luke, cooed, could, cod
4. lose, loss, lost, loose, loosed
5. crew, crude, crook, crock
6. baboon, monsoon, festoon
7. spool, pull, would, wood

[ʌ] and [ə]

The symbol [ʌ] represents the vowel sound in *but* [bʌt]. The symbol [ə], called the *schwa,* is the sound of *a* in *approve* [ə'pruv]. Although the articulation of the two sounds is somewhat similar, [ə] appears *only* in unaccented syllables.

Exercise 2.6

Transcribe the following words:

1. bun, blood, fussed, flux
2. abet, collect, condemn, vista
3. above, conundrum, alumnus, compulsive
4. walnut, muffled, enough, son, honey
5. buck, book, boot, putt, put, pool
6. symphony, sonata, funnel, accustomed

Exercise 2.7

Read the following transcriptions aloud, then write down the words they represent. Some may have more than one spelling.

1. [kə'kɑfənI, 'ɑrIə, 'lʌvəbəl, 'dæmzəl]
2. [kə'dɛnzə, bə'sun, 'ɑpərə, kwɑr'tɛt]
3. [ˌrɛsItə'tiv, ˌkʌlərə'turə, kən'klusIv]
4. ['ɔrgən, rʌf, kɔf, 'hIkəp, 'ɔfəl]
5. ['rɔkəs, du, luz, fUl'fIl]
6. [brUk, wUlvz, lus, bru, 'krUkId]
7. [lɔrd, lɑrd, hUk, hɑk, hɔk]
8. [sɔt, sUt, sɑt, sæt, sɛt]
9. [ɛg'zɔst, bI'kɔz, fɑks, kɔt]

Diphthongs

The word *diphthong* comes from the Greek *di-,* two, and *phthongos,* sound. A diphthong is a vowel which begins with one sound and ends with another.

Although only two of the English diphthongs are regularly spelled with two vowels, there are at least five diphthongs in English.

[ɔI] and [aU]

The diphthong [ɔI] is the vowel sound in *boy* [bɔI].

The diphthong [aU] is the vowel sound in *how* [haU]. Notice that we use the symbol [a] instead of the symbol [ɑ] for the first part of the diphthong. The pronunciation of the sounds [a] and [ɑ] will be discussed below.

Exercise 2.8

Transcribe the following words:

1. bough, boy, boil, bout
2. decoy, ploy, plough, exploit
3. abound, anoint, foist, Faust, clown
4. fowl, foul, foil, fool, full, folly, fun
5. crowd, proud, about, royal

[aI, eI, oU]

There are three other sounds which must be considered phonetically as diphthongs even though they are commonly assumed to be single sounds. These are [aI] as in *pile* [paIl], [eI] as in *pale* [peIl], and [oU] as in *pole* [poUl]. Of course, these diphthongs have a variety of spellings, including some which apparently have a letter to represent the second element [I] or [U], such as *i* in *maid* [meId] or *w* in *low* [loU]. It is important to realize that there is no distinction in pronunciation between the vowel in *maid* and that in *made* and that both must be transcribed with the diphthong [eI].

Exercise 2.9

Transcribe the following words:

1. ways, weighs, wades, waits, straight
2. load, lode, lowed, dough, mouldy
3. write, right, slight, sleight, slate
4. height, weight, receive, weird
5. stole, stale, stile, style, steel
6. great, gray, mind, guide, aisle
7. sew, know, ago, sorrow, window

Exercise 2.10

Read the following transcriptions aloud, then write the words they represent. Some may have more than one spelling.

1. ['lɔIəl, ə'baUt, sleI, veIn, roUd]
2. [aIl, laI, rI'freIn, roUm, rum, rʌm]

3. [taɪm, 'mɛdoU, loUn, 'kwaɪət, oU, aU]
4. [baɪd, boUd, beɪd, baUd, bɔɪd, bid, bɪd, bæd, bɔd, bɛd, bud, bʌd]
5. ['soUfə, aɪ, reɪn, kəm'pleɪn, soUl]

English Diphthong versus German Monophthong

With the sounds [eɪ] and [oU], it is very important to be aware of the second elements [ɪ] and [U]. In English, except in some unaccented syllables, these sounds always appear as diphthongs and never as the monophthongs [e] and [o]. In German, as well as in other major European languages, these sounds always appear as monophthongs. Contrast the following:

English	German
bait [beɪt]	Beet [bet]
boat [boUt]	Boot [bot]

To pronounce the German words with the English vowels would result in a recognizable, and undesirable, accent. We will treat these sounds in greater detail in Chapter 6.

[ɑ] versus [a]

In the diphthongs [aɪ] and [aU], a new symbol, [a], is introduced. Though the sound it represents does not occur in isolation in standard American English, it can be isolated for the sake of contrast by pronouncing *lie* [laɪ] and eliminating the second element of the diphthong: [la]. The sound thus obtained is quite different from the sound in *la* [lɑ], [ɑ] being more of a back vowel and [a] being more of a front vowel. The sound [a] does exist in isolation in some accents, for example, in the New England pronunciation of *Harvard* ['havəd] or in the Deep South pronunciation of *dry wine* [dra wan]. The two sounds do occur in isolation in German, although the differentiation is made more in speaking than in singing. This will be discussed further in Chapter 9.

CONSONANTS

The symbols for most consonant sounds are the same as the letters of the alphabet most commonly used to represent the sounds. Some letters, however, have more than one pronunciation, and certain groups of letters represent a single sound. In both cases, some new symbols are required to represent the sounds.

[j]

Although phoneticians are not in agreement on the classification of [j] and [w], calling them variously *semivowels* or *glides,* these sounds are treated in this text as consonants. The symbol [j] represents the sound of *y* in *yes* [jɛs] or the initial element of *u* in *use* [juz] or *fuse* [fjuz]. The sound has other spellings, which are illustrated in the following exercise.

Exercise 2.11   Transcribe the following words:

1. Yale, yak, yen, yield, yoke, yacht, yawl, yule
2. hue, hew, human, view, cute
3. beautiful, onion, music, accurate
4. due, news, neutral, suit, tune, consume
5. euphoria, feudal, futile, stew, stupid

[ŋ]

The symbol [ŋ] represents the sound of *ng* in *tang* [tæŋ] and *n* in *tank* [tæŋk]. Note that in the combination *ng, g* is sometimes pronounced, sometimes not, e.g., *finger* ['fɪŋgər], *singer* ['sɪŋər].

Exercise 2.12   Transcribe the following words:

1. swinging, fang, long, lung
2. sink, sank, sunk
3. hungry, angry, single, longer
4. ankle, inkling, donkey, monkey, uncle
5. concord, concubine, conclave, conquer
6. ingot, ingrate, pancake, spank

[ʃ] and [ʒ]

The symbol [ʃ] represents the sound of *sh* in *shot* [ʃɑt] or *ti* of the syllable *-tion,* as in *nation* ['neɪʃən]. The symbol [ʒ] represents the sound of *s* in pleasure ['plɛʒər] or *si* in *Asia* ['eɪʒə]. Both sounds have other spellings, which are illustrated in the following exercise.

Exercise 2.13   Transcribe the following words:

1. shad, shade, shed, shod, should, shied
2. passion, machine, fiction, fashion, fascist, sugar, issue, ocean, special
3. treasure, confusion, occasion, decision, prestige, garage
4. fusion, fission, fissure, concussion, glacier, glazier

Exercise 2.14   Read the following transcriptions aloud, then write the words they represent. Some may have more than one spelling.

1. [ˈeɪnʃənt, ˈæʒur, du, dju, jʌŋ]
2. [ˈmɛʒər, ˈmoʊʃən, ruz, ruʒ]
3. [ˈsiˌʃɛl, ˌʃɪpˈʃeɪp, ˈkɪŋdəm, ˈʃæloʊ]
4. [ˈwɪŋɪd, ˈjɛloʊ, jild, ʃip, jɪr]

[tʃ] and [dʒ]

The combined symbol [tʃ] represents the sound of *ch* in *chat* [tʃæt]; [dʒ] represents the sound of *j* in *joy* [dʒɔɪ]. Both sounds have other spellings.

Exercise 2.15   Transcribe the following words:

1. chants, chance, choke, choice, cheek
2. catch, ketch, cello
3. jam, judge, bridge, gem
4. batch, badge, just, gust, gist, jest
5. char, jar, ridge, rich, garage

[ɾ]

The symbol [ɾ] is used to represent the sound of *r* in the stereotypical English butler's "very [vɛɾɪ] good, sir." The sound, which is also represented by *rr*, is called a *one-tap trill.* Although this pronunciation is usually said to occur between vowels, very few Americans use it in that position, preferring instead [r]. In actual practice, the American articulation of *t, tt* and *d, dd* between vowels is virtually indistinguishable from [ɾ]; thus *catty, caddy,* and *carry* might all be pronounced [ˈkæɾɪ], although convention dictates that we transcribe *t* or *tt* as [t] and *d* or *dd* as [d].

One position in which many Americans use the pronunciation [ɾ] for *r* is after *th.* If the words *three, throw* are pronounced quickly and forcefully, the one-tap trill can be clearly heard.

It is beyond the scope of this text to consider the significance of [ɾ] in singing English. This pronunciation of *r* is very important in German diction, however, and will be discussed in greater detail in Chapters 5 and 12.

[θ] and [ð]

The symbol [θ] represents the sound of *th* in *thin* [θɪn]. The symbol [ð] represents the sound of *th* in *then* [ðɛn].

Exercise 2.16   Transcribe the following words:

1. this, that, think, thin
2. thrift, three, brother, bother
3. wrath, rather, cloth, clothing

4. father, path, paths, pithy

5. throng, faith, Gothic, goatherd

Exercise 2.17

Read the following transcriptions aloud, then write the words they represent. Some may have more than one spelling:

1. ['weɪdʒər, wɪtʃ, 'ʃɛpərd, 'rɛtʃɪd, rɛkt]
2. [hɛɪld, 'twaɪˌlaɪt, ɛk'spɪrɪəns, 'prɑmptlɪ]
3. ['fɑðər, ə'nʌðər, 'tʃɑrmɪŋ, reɪndʒd, tʌŋz]
4. [juθ, dʒus, 'ærɪ, hɛlθ, 'θʌndrəs]
5. [strɛtʃ, 'freɪgrənt, 'stɛlθɪlɪ, baʊz]
6. [θrɛd, θrʌst, 'blasəmz, 'mɪst, 'bʊzəm]
7. ['paɪəs, 'prɪði, 'eɪndʒəl, rɪ'dʒɔɪs]
8. [ˌfær'wɛl, sɔŋz, 'θaʊzənd, 'rʌʃɪŋ, dʒu'dɪʃəs]
9. [ðaɪn, tɪtʃ, hɑrt, eɪk, 'nʌθɪŋ, mjut]
10. [ɑrtʃt, dɛpθ, boʊθ, tʃɔɪs, ðoʊ]

Chapter 3 | Describing Sounds: Articulatory Phonetics

When learning the sounds of another language, it is desirable to describe the mechanical means by which sounds are formed. If a sound is articulated differently from its English analog, what do we do with our tongue, teeth, and lips to reflect this difference? The study of how sounds are produced is called articulatory phonetics.

It is logical to begin the study of articulatory phonetics by analyzing the sounds of one's own language, since the student can produce the sounds naturally and correctly and can then determine by feel how the speech apparatus is being employed to produce them. Having thus become consciously aware of the speech apparatus, the student can learn to control it and use it to produce unfamiliar sounds.

Appendix A on p. 156 contains charts which provide complete phonetic descriptions of each vowel and consonant. Refer to them for orientation, but do not memorize the descriptions. The main objective of this chapter is to make you aware of how you use your speech apparatus to produce sounds. Rote learning of phonetic descriptions will probably not help you toward this objective.

CONSONANTS

Although there is no universal agreement on just what a consonant is, we will adhere to a more or less traditional classification. A fairly complete description of the production of a consonant sound can be given with three items of information:

1. voicing
2. major articulator(s)
3. manner of production

The sound [b], for example, is described as a *voiced bilabial stop*.

Voicing

When the vocal chords vibrate during the production of a sound, for example [z], the sound is said to be *voiced*. When they do not vibrate, as in the production of [s], the sound is said to be *voiceless*.

Exercise 3.1

Indicate whether the underlined letters in the following words represent voiced or voiceless consonants. Refer to the chart in Appendix A only to check yourself.

1. ton	12. pats
2. den	13. pads
3. bed	14. boxes
4. bet	15. vision
5. pad	16. fission
6. bad	17. edge
7. his	18. etch
8. this	19. rag
9. thistle	20. rack
10. bath	21. win
11. baths	

Articulators

Figure 1 identifies the main apparatus for producing speech sounds. The second of the three terms used in the description of a consonant sound indicates the major articulator(s) involved in its production. Below is a list of such terms. The role of the tongue is not normally reflected in the descriptive term.

Figure 1. Points of Articulation

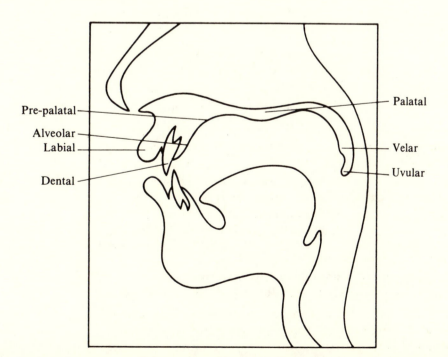

Bilabial   A bilabial consonant involves the use of both lips to stop or constrict the flow of breath, for example, [b] or [w].

Labiodental   A labiodental consonant involves the upper teeth and lower lip in its production, for example, [f].

Dental   In articulating a dental consonant, the tip of the tongue is brought into contact with the back of the upper teeth, as in [θ].

Alveolar   An alveolar consonant involves the tip or blade of the tongue and the alveolar ridge in its production, as in [n] or [s].

Pre-palatal   A pre-palatal consonant involves the tip or blade of the tongue and the area between the alveolar ridge and the hard palate, for example, [r] or [ʒ].

Palatal   A palatal consonant is produced with the blade of the tongue and the hard palate, as in [j].

Velar   A velar consonant is formed with the back of the tongue and the velum, or soft palate, for example, [k] or [ŋ]. Sometimes, especially in reference to German, the velar consonants are called *guttural* consonants.

Glottal   The glottis is the opening between the vocal chords. It is almost closed in the production of the glottal consonant [h].

Exercise 3.2   Describe the sounds represented by the underlined letters with one of the above terms.

1. ball	11. fission
2. cat	12. laser
3. vision	13. find
4. nut	14. thin
5. tip	15. ton
6. wolf	16. bad
7. think	17. volt
8. dog	18. mama
9. hot	19. rip
10. yes	20. paths

Manner of Production

In the preceding section we discussed the apparatus involved in producing speech sounds. We now need to describe how the apparatus is used to produce the sounds. Although [t] and [s] may both be described as alveolar and voiceless, it is clear that we are using the same apparatus to do two quite different things.

Below is a list of terms which describe the manner in which consonant sounds are produced.

Stop   In the production of a stop, all air flow is stopped momentarily by a set of articulators and then released, as in [b] or [k]. Stops are also called *plosives*.

Fricative A fricative is the type of sound produced by directing the air flow past a set of articulators without stopping it as in [s], [v], or [θ]. Fricatives are sometimes also called *spirants*. The s-like fricatives [s], [z], [ʃ], and [ʒ] are occasionally referred to as *sibilants*.

Affricate An affricate is a consonant sound consisting of two sounds spoken rapidly together, for example, [tʃ] and [dʒ]. An affricate consists of a stop which is released as a fricative.

Nasal In the production of a nasal, the flow of air is directed through the nasal passages, as in [m] or [ŋ].

Lateral In the production of a lateral, the air flow is directed over the sides of the tongue, as in [1].

Glide The English glides are [w] and [j]. It was pointed out above that the definition of a consonant is problematic. The glides, which are sometimes called semivowels, are part of the problem. If the student pronounces the word *we*, he will notice that it consists of a very brief [u] followed by [i]. The sounds [w] and [j] fail certain tests for vowels, however, and will be classified in this text as consonants.

Retroflex A retroflex sound is produced with the tip of the tongue curled back, as in English [r].

Trill A trill is the rapid contact between the tip of the tongue and the alveolar ridge or between the uvula and the back of the tongue. In singing, only the former type is considered. English has only the one-tap trill [ɾ]. In other languages, notably Italian, this [ɾ] may be trilled a number of times in rapid succession, producing the trill [r].[1]

Exercise 3.3	Using the above terms, give the manner of production for the sounds represented by the underlined letters.

1. pot	11. vision
2. school	12. blizzard
3. vat	13. rash
4. that	14. thrash
5. man	15. dun
6. sank	16. dug
7. fin	17. bell
8. fission	18. yet
9. kitchen	19. wolf
10. chair	20. rigid

[1] Additional terminology:

Aspiration Aspiration generally refers to the puff of air that follows a consonant, e.g., [p,t,k] in English or German. In the Romance languages, this aspiration is usually absent.

Liquid The consonants *l* and *r* are sometimes referred to as liquids, regardless of articulation.

Exercise 3.4

Write the IPA symbol for the sounds described as follows:

1. voiced bilabial stop
2. voiced dental fricative
3. voiceless velar stop
4. voiced alveolar nasal
5. voiced palatal glide
6. voiceless alveolar fricative

Exercise 3.5

Give complete, three-part descriptions of the sounds represented by the underlined letters.

1. spot	7. visible
2. pithy	8. fission
3. three	9. fusion
4. think	10. bell
5. dim	11. reef
6. wet	12. feel

VOWELS

Defining a vowel can be problematic because one has some latitude in deciding what criteria to use in arriving at a definition. This text will sidestep the question and accept the traditional division of vowels and consonants with a caution to the student that in some ways and in some instances this division is almost arbitrary.

Vowel Description

In the pronunciation of vowels, the tongue is usually in an arched position with the tip pointing down. Although the entire tongue changes position in pronouncing different vowels, it is convenient to use the position of the peak, or highest point, of the tongue arch in describing vowel sounds. Figure 2 shows the shape of the arch for certain vowels, with the dot indicating the peak for each.

If we now consider the peaks alone, we see that they can be arranged schematically as in Figure 3. From Figures 2 and 3 it can be seen that [i, e, ɛ, a][2] are arranged roughly along a line sloping upward toward the front of the mouth and that [u, o, ɔ, ɑ] are arranged roughly along a line sloping less sharply upward toward the back of the mouth, the whole configuration vaguely suggesting the form of a trapezoid which has [i, a, ɑ, u], called the cardinal

---

[2] You will recall that the sounds [e, a, o] do not commonly occur in isolation but only in the diphthongs [eI, aI, aU, oU] in standard American English. They do, however, occur in isolation in German.

Figure 2. Tongue Position for Vowels

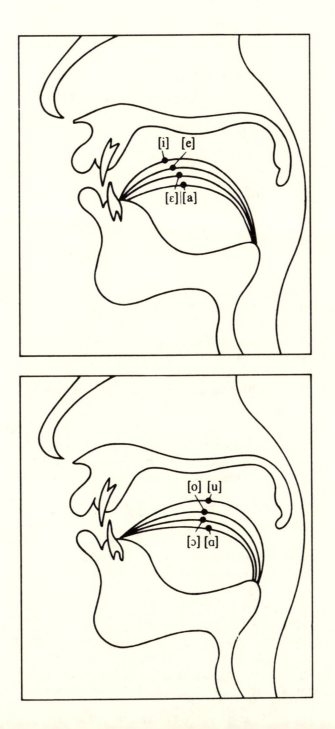

Figure 3.   Schematic Position of Peak of Tongue Arch

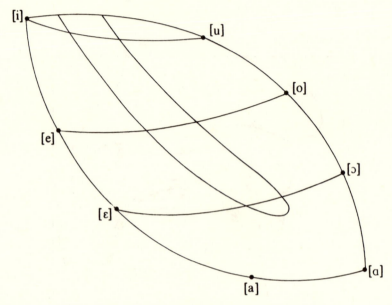

vowels, as its corners (see Figure 4). For the sake of reference, it is convenient to arrange all the vowels within or along the boundaries of a trapezoid, as in Appendix A, Chart 3.

From Appendix A, Chart 3, we see that we can pinpoint the position of the peak of the arched tongue in somewhat the same manner as we locate a point on a grid, by giving its horizontal position (front, central, back) and its vertical position (high, mid, low). Thus we see that [i] may be described as a *high front vowel.*

Exercise 3.6   Describe the vowel sounds represented by the underlined letters according to the above terminology. Use the chart in Appendix A only to check yourself.

1. keyed
2. kid
3. cad
4. cod
5. cawed
6. could
7. cooed
8. cud
9. cadenza

Quality

Another factor must be considered in the description of a vowel, in addition to tongue position. This is known as *tension* or *closeness.* The difference between [i] and [I], for example, lies not only in the fact that for [I] the tongue is drawn further down and back. In the production of [i] the muscles of the lips and tongue are under tension. With [I], the lips and tongue are more relaxed.

Figure 4. Cardinal Vowels

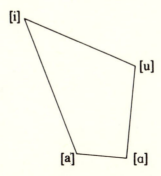

The vowel [i] is said to be *tense,* or *closed,* the vowel [I] is *lax,* or *open.* (Although *tense* and *lax* are more descriptive terms, this text will use *closed* and *open* since these terms are traditionally used in describing German vowels.) The contrast can be felt physcially by placing the finger lightly on the chin or by placing the thumb on the tongue muscle under the lower jaw and pronouncing the two sounds in succession. The following are contrasting pairs of vowels:

Front		**Back**	
closed	*open*	*closed*	*open*
i	I	u	U
e	ε	o	ɔ

It is important to understand the distinction between closed and open vowels because it plays an important role in German diction.

Exercise 3.7

Identify the vowels in the following words as closed or open:

1. wooed, would, full, fool, push
2. hole, hall, code, cawed, home
3. bet, bait, wade, wed, pen
4. seat, sit, list, leased, seize
5. frost, pose, pill, do, vault

Part Two | The Sounds of German

Chapter 4 | Introduction

In many respects, German is a very easy language to pronounce for speakers of English. It, like Italian, is commonly said to be a "phonetic" language; that is, for each spelling there are normally no more than one or two pronunciations and, conversely, for each pronunciation there are usually no more than one or two spellings. Contrast this situation with English, which has, as we pointed out above, at least ten spellings for the sound [i] and at least six pronunciations for the letter *a*.

Even when there are two pronunciations for a letter in German, it is fairly easy for the singer to recognize from the position of the letter in the word and from the letters following it which pronunciation is to be chosen. In some instances it will be necessary to recognize certain prefixes or verb endings in order to choose the right pronunciation.

ORGANIZATION

Since German is a fairly phonetic language and since one of the singer's main objectives in a study of German diction is to learn to pronounce German words printed in a score, the arrangement in this book is based on *spellings*—written symbols—rather than on sounds. Thus, even though *c* and *z* or *ie* and *i* may sometimes be pronounced alike, they are treated in different sections.

This text departs from the traditional approach of treating vowels and consonants completely separately. It instead treats the letters and their pronunciations in the order of decreasing difficulty. The difficult consonants *ch* and *r* are treated first, then the difficult closed and open vowels will be discussed. The treatment of vowels will be followed by a discussion of word structure necessary for the differentiation of sounds, and then concluding chapters on vowels and consonants will be presented.

STANDARD REFERENCE

The student of German diction is fortunate in having at his disposal a definitive reference work designed for use by professional German actors, singers, and announcers. It is *Siebs, Deutsche Hochsprache* published by Walter de Gruyter

& Co. Any college or university library will have a copy and the serious student should acquire a personal copy from the outset. *Siebs* provides pronunciations in IPA transcription of most German words and foreign words common to German, as well as transcriptions of a large number of proper names. In general, this book will follow *Siebs,* but in a few instances it departs from the transcriptions in *Siebs* for the sake of greater clarity.

GENERAL RULES

Before beginning a detailed discussion of German sounds, the singer should become familiar with a few general rules regarding pronunciation and orthography.

Pronunciation Like English In general, the singer may assume that the following consonants are pronounced as in English: *b, ck, d, f, g, h, k, m, n, p, t, x.* Exceptions will be discussed under the individual consonants.

Double Consonants In German, unlike Italian, double consonants are generally pronounced the same as single consonants, although there are notable exceptions to this rule.

Unvoicing The voiced consonants *b, d, g, s* are usually unvoiced in final position or before a consonant, for instance, *d* in *Bad* [bɑt], *g* in *legt* [lekt].

Word Structure The division of words into their component parts can affect vowel quality and unvoicing, as well as the pronunciation of double consonants and consonant clusters. Word structure is discussed further in Chapter 7.

Capitalization The student will note that many words in the following examples and exercises are capitalized. In German, all nouns are capitalized, including common nouns such as *Baum* (tree), *Geist* (spirit), etc.

Umlaut The umlaut letters *ä, ö, ü* are also spelled *ae, oe, ue* in some scores. There is no difference in pronunciation.

Chapter 5 | The Sounds of *r, ch*

It is well to begin the treatment of German pronunciation with the difficult consonants *r* and *ch*. The exercises in subsequent chapters can then include these consonants and provide ongoing practice in them. A review and conclusion of the sounds discussed in this chapter will be found in Chapters 12 and 15.

SECTION 1: *r, rr*

Speaking versus Singing

In speaking, the pronunciation of *r* before a vowel is uvular, that is, it involves contact between the far back part of the tongue and the uvula, producing a gargling sound. The uvular pronunciation (IPA [R]) is used in singing popular songs but should be avoided in art songs and opera. The one-tap trill, or flipped *r* [ɾ], should be used instead.

In other positions, the pronunciation of *r* in speaking is more vowel-like in quality. The conditions for the use of this latter pronunciation in singing are not as clearly defined as those for most German sounds, and the singer is left a certain amount of latitude in its use.

Prevocalic: [ɾ]

The letter *r* should generally be pronounced as a one-tap trill when it stands before a vowel: *raten* ['rɑtən] (guess), *beraten* [bə'rɑtən] (advise). (Apparent exceptions to this rule are covered in Chapters 7 and 12.)

In non-compound words, *rr* should be pronounced the same as *r: Karre* ['kɑrə] (cart) (see also Chapter 12).

The singer should take care to tap the tongue only once against the alveolar ridge. Some singers occasionally roll this trill as for the Italian or Spanish *rr*. In German diction, this articulation should be avoided at first. Any decision to experiment with it should be based on many hours of critical listening to established singers.

Exercise 5.1   Pronounce the following words using the one-tap trill for the *r* and *rr:*

1. Rand
   rasch
   Rest
   retten
   ringen
   Reigen
   rauschen
   Reue

2. Karre
   irren
   fahren
   ihren
   sperren
   führen
   lauere
   eure

3. aufragen
   Abreise
   Hauptrolle
   bereue
   gerissen

4. fragen
   Kragen
   tragen
   dreist
   graben
   Preis
   Schrift
   bringen

Final Position in Some Words and Syllables: [ɒ][1]

The alternate pronunciation of *r* is in effect a vowel sound which can be viewed as a variant of schwa [ə]. The tongue is drawn back a little further than for schwa, producing a back vowel which is very close to the sound of *o* in the British pronunciation of *hot* [hɒt]. In the articulation of schwa, the tip of the tongue is normally pointed down. In the articulation of [ɒ], the tongue should be pointed at, but not touching, the alveolar ridge. In this manner, the relationship of [ɒ] to the one-tap trill [ɾ] is maintained and the articulations may be easily interchanged, as style requires.

There are no hard and fast rules on when to use [ɒ]. Indeed, some singers almost never use it, and until recently this pronunciation was all but ignored by the authorities on the subject. However, most singers now make judicious use of [ɒ], especially in the nineteenth-century art song. As a rule of thumb, let us say that *r* will be pronounced [ɒ] in one-syllable articles, pronouns, adverbs, and prepositions such as *der, mir, wir, ihr, nur, vor, für* as well as in the prefixes *er-, ver-,* and *zer-*. Other than in these cases and in the suffix *-er* (see next paragraph), *r* is generally pronounced as a one-tap trill. The trill may of course be used in any position; however, the voice student is urged to practice the vocalic pronunciation [ɒ] in the positions listed here. A further discussion of *r* will be found in Chapter 12.

[1] Most references do not differentiate between the two types of *r*, using the symbol [r] for both. However, the singer is urged to adopt both [ɾ] and [ɒ] in his notation in order to reflect the difference in articulation.

The Suffix *-er:* [ɒ]

In accordance with the previous section, *r* is given the pronunciation [ɒ] in *der* [deɒ] (the) or *wir* [viɒ] (we), and the preceding vowel maintains its integrity. In the suffix *-er,* however, *e* and *r* are articulated together as [ɒ], as in *bitter* ['bItɒ] (bitter). This suffix may also occur before other suffixes or endings beginning with consonants, as in *bitterster* ['bItɒstɒ] (bitterest) or in verb forms such as *flattern* ['flɑtɒn] (flutter), *wandern* ['vɑndɒn] (wander).

The suffix *-er* should not be confused with the prefix *er-,* which is always pronounced [ɛɒ], as in *erfahren* [ɛɒ'fɑrən] (experience).

Other Positions: [ɾ]

In positions other than those described above, *r* should be pronounced as the one-tap trill [ɾ] (see Chapter 12).

Exercise 5.2	Pronounce the following words, using [ɒ] for the suffix *-er* and for *r* in the recommended syllables and prefixes:

1. der, wer, mir, ihr, wir
2. erfahren, erkennen, verkleiden, derselbe, versagen
3. Lieder, leider, Vater, Meistersinger, Wagner, Wiener, immer, besser, Musiker, Orchester, Walter, Ritter, Retter, Wunder, Kindergarten
4. wandern, wanderst, wandert, wanderten, verbessert, mildert, flatterte, bitterlich

Exercise 5.3	Final *e* is pronounced [ə] in German (see Chapter 6, section 3). Practice contrasting [ə] and [ɒ] in the following pairs:

1.	Messe	Messer
2.	spiele	Spieler
3.	gute	guter
4.	Liede	Lieder
5.	Leide	leider
6.	Liebe	lieber
7.	Treue	treuer
8.	meiste	Meister
9.	singe	Singer
10.	blaue	blauer

Exercise 5.4	Transcribe the following words into the IPA, using [ɾ] or [ɒ]:

1. Lieder, Bier, Rest, Retter, Kraft
2. Ritter, wandern, irren, Schubert, Bruckner

Excerpt

Read the following passage aloud, paying special attention to the pronunciation of *r:*

So wie dort in blauer Tiefe,
Hell und herrlich, jener Stern,
Also er an meinem Himmel,
Hell und herrlich, hoch und fern.

Frauenliebe und Leben
Schumann

SECTION 2: *ch*

There are two distinctly different pronunciations of *ch,* which should never be confused with each other.

[χ]

The sound [χ] is a voiceless velar fricative, a heavily aspirated [h], as in *Bach* [bɑχ]. This pronunciation of *ch* occurs after *a, o, u,* and *au.*

Exercise 5.5

Pronounce the following words using [χ] for *ch:*

1. ach	2. noch	4. Buch
machen	doch	Kuchen
Pracht		suchen
nach	3. auch	
Nacht	Rauch	
gemacht	Raucher	

[ç]

The sound [ç] is a voiceless palatal fricative. The tongue is in the same position as for [j], but air is passed over it, producing a hissing sound. The sound is very much like the initial sound in the words *hue, huge,* and *human,* as pronounced in standard American. (In many areas, however, especially in some large cities, the fricative element at the beginning of these words is lost.) The pronunciation [ç] is used in German after all vowels other than *a, o, u, au,* as well as after consonants.

Other pronunciations for *ch* will be treated in the conclusion of the discussion of *ch* in Chapter 15.

Exercise 5.6

Pronounce the following words, using [ç] for *ch:*

1. rächen	2. nicht	3. mancher	4. schnarchen
Becher	Angesicht	Milch	Lerche
brechen	schleichen	welcher	Liebchen
riechen	Eiche	Kelch	Männchen
ich	euch		
mich	feucht		

Exercise 5.7

Transcribe the following words into the IPA (*ä* = [ɛ]):

1. ich, ach, Becher, nicht, Nacht, Nächte, Bach, Bäche

2. Kuchen, Milch, schnarchen, Eiche, riechen

Excerpt

Read the following passage aloud, paying special attention to the pronunciation of *ch.* Note: *ä* = [ɛ]; *v* = [f]; and *eu* = [ɔI]—approximately (see Chapter 11)

Kommt das grämliche Gesicht,
Kommt die Alte da mit Keuchen,
Lieb' und Lust mir zu verscheuchen,
Eh' die Jugend mir gebricht?
Ach! die Mutter ist's die aufwacht,
Und den Mund zu schelten aufmacht,
Nein, die Karten lügen nicht!

Die Kartenlegerin
Schumann

Tape

Practice speaking the text of the following song until you can read it through without errors. Then make a tape recording of the text. Do not stop the machine while recording; if you make a mistake, start over. Note: *st* = [ʃt]; *äu, eu* = [ɔI] (approximately); *z* = [ts].

Song

Sing the following song in class. Pay very careful attention to the contrasts [r]:[ɒ] and [χ]:[ç].

Am Brunnen vor dem Tore

Am Brun-nen vor dem To - re da steht ein Lin-den -
Ich musst' auch heu-te wan-dern vor-bei in tie-fer
Die kal-ten Win-de blie-sen mir grad ins An-ge -

baum, ich träumt' in sein-em Schat-ten so man-chen sü - ssen
Nacht, da hab ich noch im Dun-keln die Au-gen zu-ge -
sicht; der Hut flog mir vom Kop-fe, ich wen-de-te____ mich

Traum; ich schnitt in sei-ne Rin - de so man-ches lie-be
macht; und sei-ne Zwei-ge rausch-ten als rie - fen sie mir
nicht. Nun bin ich man-che Stun-de ent-fernt von je-nem

Wort,   es zog in Freud und Lei - de zu
zu: Komm her zu mir Ge - sel - le, hier
Ort,   und im mer hör ichs rau - schen: Du

ihm___ mich im - mer fort, zu ihm___ mich im - mer fort.
findst___ du dei - ne Ruh, hier findst___ du dei - ne Ruh.
fän - dest Ru - he dort, du fän - dest Ru - he dort.

Chapter 6 | Closed or Open Monophthongs

DIPHTHONGIZATION

In Chapter 2, it was pointed out that the English vowels generally assumed to be monophthongs frequently have a diphthongal element. This is almost universally true of the vowels long *a* [eI] and long *o* [oU]. It is also true of other vowels to a greater or lesser extent, depending on regional accent. One frequently hears reference to the "purity" of vowels in European languages. By this "purity" is meant the absence of the diphthongal elements characteristic of some English vowels. Thus the pronunciation of the English word *Dane* [deIn] is by no means the same as that for the German word *den* [den] (the).

Practice the contrast between English and German vowels in the following pairs of words. You will note that for the English diphthong sounds the jaw moves slightly during the pronunciation of the vowel. For the German sound, concentrate on holding the jaw in one position while articulating the vowel. For many speakers, a number of the words will be pronounced the same in English and in German.

Exercise 6.1

Contrast:

English	German	
bate	Beet	(flowerbed)
lame	Lehm	(mud)
lone	Lohn	(wage)
tote	tot	(dead)
toot	tut	(does)
geese	giess	(pour)
puts	Putz	(finery)
bet	Bett	(bed)
pest	Pest	(pestilence)
mitt	mit	(with)
bin	bin	(am)

QUALITY

In Chapter 3, we discussed the distinction between closed, tense vowels and open, lax vowels. German monophthongs can be classified as either open or closed. Except for *a* [ɑ] and *ä* [ɛ], which are generally considered always open, we can say that *long* vowels are *closed* and that *short* vowels are *open*. Thus the monophthongs discussed in this chapter—*i, ü* (and *y*), *e, ö, o,* and *u*—will be closed in some positions and open in others.

LENGTH

The singer is spared some of the headache of learning German vowels encountered by the regular student of German. In speaking, a long vowel is actually extended to about double the duration of a short vowel. In singing, of course, the length of the vowel is largely determined by the length of the note on which it is sung. We will therefore focus on the difference in *quality* between long and short vowels rather than on the difference in length.

The singer should be aware that a long German vowel is indicated in IPA transcription by placing a colon after it, for example, [e:]. Although this notation is common in reference works and other textbooks, it will not generally be used in this text.

This will spare the singer the effort of indicating quantitative length in transcriptions. In the case of *a* and *ä,* which make no *qualitative* distinction between the long and the short vowel, this will be particularly time-saving since these vowels exhibit a sizable number of exceptions to the rules on length.

RULES ON LENGTH AND QUALITY

The vowels of this chapter—*i, ü* (and *y*), *e, ö, o,* and *u* (and only these vowels!)—may be either long and closed or short and open, depending on certain conditions[1]:

Rule 1. Any of these vowels followed by *h* is long and closed. Normally, the *h* following an accented vowel is not pronounced, even if it precedes another vowel (see also Chapter 13).

Exercise 6.2   Pronounce:

1. stehlen	2. stehen
ihn	drohen
ohne	Ruhe
Ruhm	Flöhe
stöhnen	Brühe
rühren	

[1] The rules stated here affect both the length and the quality of the monophthongs discussed in this chapter. They also affect the *length* of *a* and *ä;* but since in singing, at any rate, the quality of *a* and *ä* are not affected by these rules they will not be considered here.

Rule 2. The double vowels *ee* and *oo* are long and closed.[2]

Exercise 6.3   Pronounce:

Beet
Meer
Boot
Moor

Rule 3. Before consonants, the vowels of this chapter may be long and closed or short and open.

a. When these vowels are followed by a single consonant, they are usually long and closed. Common exceptions to this rule, such as *in* and *von,* will be covered in the sections below.

Exercise 6.4   Pronounce:

Reben	schuf
Weg	Muse
wider	öde
Boden	übel
bog	

b. When these vowels are followed by more than one consonant, they are nearly always short and open. There are common exceptions to this rule, especially before the combinations *ss, ch, st,* and *r + dental.* These will be listed in the sections below.

Exercise 6.5   Pronounce:

denn	bunt
Ring	Hölle
Knospe	Lüfte

In compounds, in words containing prefixes, and in inflected forms, a basic knowledge of German word structure is necessary to recognize whether a vowel is followed by one consonant or more than one consonant. This subject is pursued in some detail in Chapter 7 and should be considered an integral part of these rules concerning length.

SECTION 1: *i*

[i]

Long and closed [i] is pronounced about like *i* in English *machine.* It occurs regularly before *h* as in *ihn* [in] (him) or before a single consonant as in *mir* [miɒ] (me).

---

[2] The only other vowel that occurs doubled is *aa,* which is always open—see Chapter 9.

Exercise 6.6	Pronounce:

1. ihm	2. wider	3. mir
ihr	Titel	wir
ihn	Bibel	Appetit
ihnen	Tiger	Kredit

[I]

Short and open [I] is pronounced about like *i* in English *pick*. It occurs regularly before two or more consonants as in *bist* [bIst] (are).

Exercise 6.7	Pronounce:

1. bitte	2. Wirt
spricht	wird
ich	irdisch
dich	irgend
Kind	Kirsche
ist	Kirche
bist	

Exceptions[3]

1. In certain words, *i* is open before a single consonant. Memorize these:

in, im	(in, in the)
bin	(am)
mit	(with)
April	(April)
hin	(there)

2. In some suffixes ending in a single consonant, *i* is always open. Memorize these suffixes:

   -in
   -nis
   -ig (pronounced [Iç])

Exercise 6.8	Pronounce:

1. Studentin	2. Ärgernis	3. fertig
Feindin	Kenntnis	giftig
Ärztin	Gefängnis	Käfig
Berlinerin		
Engländerin		

---

[3] Many of the exceptions listed in this book may appear in various compounds; for example *in* also appears in *darin, worin*, etc.—*mit* appears in *damit, mitgehen, mithin*, etc. Except as otherwise noted, the pronunciation of the basic word remains the same.

3. In the final combination *-ik, i* is closed if the syllable is accented and open if unaccented. Memorize the following examples:

accented	*unaccented*
Musik	Chronik
Kritik	Tragik
Politik	Lyrik

Exercise 6.9

Differentiate between [i] and [I] in the following pairs:

1. wider   Widder
2. Lid   litt
3. ihnen   innen
4. Stil   still
5. Mine   Minne
6. Iren   irren

Exercise 6.10

Pronounce the following words, applying the rules for closed or open monophthongs:

1. Winter, sitzen, Igel, mir, Hirsch
2. finden, Stimme, ihn, in, bilden
3. Studentin, Bibel, Kenntnis, heilige, Mitte
4. April, Stil, Mine, hin, Titel
5. Musik, wider, Tragik, wissen, bin, mit

Exercise 6.11

Transcribe the above words into the IPA.

Excerpts

Read the following excerpts aloud, paying special attention to the pronunciation of *i:*

1. Doch bin ich, wie ich bin,
Und nimm mich nur hin!
Willst du bessre besitzen,
So lass dir sie schnitzen.
Ich bin nur, wie ich bin;
So nimm mich nur hin.

   Liebhaber in allen Gestalten
   Schubert

2. Seit ich ihn gesehen,
   Glaub ich blind zu sein;
Wo ich hin nur blicke,
   Seh' ich ihn allein.

   Frauenliebe und Leben
   Schumann

Song

Sing the following song, focusing on the contrast between [i] and [I]. Note that *ie* is usually pronounced [i].

Du, du, liegst mir im Herzen

Du,   du,   liegst mir im   Her - zen,   du,   du,
So,   so,   wie   ich dich lie - be,   so,   so,
Doch,   doch,   darf ich dir   trau - en,   dir,   dir,
Und,   und,   wenn in der   Fer - ne   mir,   mir

liegst mir im Sinn.   Du,   du,   machst mir viel Schmer-zen,
lie - be   auch mich.   Die,   die   zärt - lich-sten Trie - be
mit leicht-em Sinn?   Du,   du,   kannst auf mich   bau - en,
dein Bild er - scheint,   dann,   dann,   wünscht ich so   ger - ne,

weisst nicht wie gut ich dir   bin. _____   Ja, ja,
füh - le ich ein - zig für dich. _____   Ja, ja,
weisst ja   wie gut ich dir   bin. _____   Ja, ja,
dass uns die Lie - be ver - eint. _____   Ja, ja,

ja,   ja,   weisst nicht, wie   gut   ich   dir   bin._____
ja,   ja,   füh - le   ich   ein - zig   für   dich._____
ja,   ja,   weisst ja, wie   gut   ich   dir   bin._____
ja,   ja,   dass uns   die   Lie - be   ver - eint._____

SECTION 2: *ü, y*

The letter *ü* (also spelled *ue*) represents sounds which are variations of the sounds of *i*. The letter *y* follows the same rules for pronunciation as the letter *ü*.

[y]

Long and closed [y] is the same sound as long and closed [i] but is pronounced with the lips rounded. Pronounce an extended [i:::::] and, *without changing the position of the tongue or jaw,* slowly round the lips. Be aware that you are really pronouncing the sound [i]. For both [i] and [y] the sides of the tongue are against the upper back molars. Only the rounding of the lips makes the distinction between the two sounds. Practice alternating [i] and [y] by slowly rounding and unrounding the lips while pronouncing [i:::::].

The pronunciation of *ü* (or *y*) is regularly long and closed [y] before *h*, as in *fühlen* ['fylən] (feel), or before a single consonant, as in *für* [fyɒ] (for), *Lyrik* ['lyrɪk] (lyrics).

Exercise 6.12   Contrast the following pairs of words containing [i] and [y]:

1. Stile   Stühle
2. Lide   lüde
3. liegen   lügen
4. sieden   Süden
5. vier   für
6. Triebe   trübe
7. Miete   Mythe
8. Riemen   rühmen
9. Fliege   Flüge
10. Biene   Bühne
11. Tier   Tür

Exercise 6.13   Pronounce only the words containing *ü* in Exercise 6.12.

Exceptions

There are a few words in which *ü* is closed before two or more consonants.
Memorize these:

1. before *st* in:
   Wüste   (desert)
   düster   (somber)
2. before *ss* in:
   büssen   (atone)
   müssig   (leisurely)
   süss   (sweet)
   grüssen   (greet)
   Füsse   (feet)
3. before *ch* in:
   Bücher   (books)
   Tücher   (cloths)

[Y]

Short and open [Y] is the same sound as short and open [I], but pronounced with the lips rounded. Pronounce an extended [I:::::] and, *without changing the position of the tongue or jaw,* slowly round the lips.

The position of the tongue is the same for both [I] and [Y]. Only the rounding of the lips makes the distinction between the two sounds. Now practice alternating [I] and [Y] by slowly rounding and unrounding the lips while pronouncing [I:::::::].

Be aware that [i] and [y] are closed sounds and that [I] and [Y] are open sounds; that is, the jaw is slightly dropped and the front of the tongue is slightly lowered for the latter.

The pronunciation of *ü* and *y* is regularly short and open [Y] before two or more consonants, as in *fünf* [fYnf] (five), *idyllisch* [i'dYlIʃ] (idyllic).

Exercise 6.14   Contrast [I] and [Y] in the following pairs of words:

1. Kissen   küssen
2. Kiste   Küste
3. sticken   Stücken
4. missen   müssen
5. Gericht   Gerücht
6. ticken   Tücken
7. Minze   Münze
8. Kinde   künde

Exercise 6.15   Pronounce only the words with *ü* in the above exercise.

Exercise 6.16

Contrast closed [y] and open [Y] in the following pairs of words:

1. Wüste   wüsste
2. fühle   fülle
3. rügte   rückte
4. Flüge   flügge
5. Hüte   Hütte
6. pflügte   pflückte
7. kühnste   Künste
8. büke   bücke

Exercise 6.17

Pronounce the following words, applying the rules for closed or open monophthongs:

1. wütend, fühlen, Lyrik, Güte, Hülle, füttern
2. Münze, nützen, dürfen, Hügel, flügge, Lüfte
3. Mythe, Hymne, Analyse, Küste, Wüste, typisch
4. düster, rüsten, fünf, fürchten, für, stürzen
5. müssen, büssen, süssen, wünschen, Jünger
6. dürrer, Dürer, würde, idyllisch, grün, Gründe
7. Frühling, Rhythmus, blühen, Schüssel, flüstern

Exercise 6.18

Transcribe the above words into the IPA.

Exercise 6.19

Read the following transcriptions aloud.

1. [bə'rymt, 'bɾydɒ, 'bynə, 'flYçtIç, 'bYɾgɒ]
2. ['dɾYkən, 'dYɾə, 'kyçə, 'gɾysən, 'hytən]
3. [fɾy, 'fYtɒn, 'flygəl, 'fYlən, 'blytə]

Excerpts

Read the following excerpts aloud, paying special attention to the pronunciation of *ü:*

1. Durch tote Wüsten wandle hin,
   Und grüne Schatten breiten sich,
   Ob fürchterliche Schwüle dort
   Ohn' Ende brüte, wonnevoll.

Wie bist du, meine Königin
Brahms

2. Übern Garten durch die Lüfte
   Hört ich Wandervögel ziehn,
   Das bedeutet Frühlingsdüfte,
   Unten fängts schon an zu blühn.

Frühlingsnacht
Schumann

Song

Sing the following song, concentrating on the contrast between [y] and [Y].

So sei gegrüsst viel tausendmal

So sei ge - grüsst viel tau - send - mal, hol - der, hol - der
Du kommst und froh ist al - le Welt, hol - der, hol - der
So sei ge - grüsst viel tau - send - mal, hol - der, hol - der

Früh - ling! Will - kom - men hier in un - serm Tal,
Früh - ling! Es freut sich Wie - se Wald und Feld,
Früh - ling! O bleib recht lang in un - serm Tal,

hol - der, hol - der   Früh - ling!   Hol - der Früh - ling   ü - ber-all
hol - der, hol - der   Früh - ling!   Ju - bel tönt dir   ü - ber-all,
hol - der, hol - der   Früh - ling!   Kehr_ in al - le   Her - zen ein,

grü - ssen wir dich froh mit   Sang und Schall,   mit   Sang und Schall.
dich be-grü - sset Lerch und   Nach - ti - gall,   und   Nach - ti - gall.
lass doch al - le mit uns   fröh - lich sein,   recht   fröh - lich sein.

SECTION 3: e

[e]

Long and closed [e] is basically the first element of the English diphthong [eI], as in *gate* [geIt]. In pronouncing [eI], note how the sides of the tongue slide inward along the molars and how the tip of the tongue and the jaw rise slightly.

In articulating the German sound [e], as in *geht* [get] (goes), all movement of the tongue and jaw, and hence all trace of the English diphthongal element [I], must be avoided. First practice pronouncing an extended [e:::::], allowing no movement of tongue or jaw. Then practice pronouncing *geht*, exaggerating the length of the vowel—[ge:::::t]—and allowing the tip of the tongue to rise only when articulating the [t].

The pronunciation of *e* is regularly long and closed [e]: (1) when it occurs in an accented syllable before *h: gehen* ['geən] (go) (see also Chapter 13); (2) when it occurs doubled: *Beet* [bet] (flowerbed); and (3) when it occurs before a single consonant: *beten* ['betən] (pray).

Exercise 6.20 Pronounce the following words containing [e]:

1. Weh	2. Beet
stehlen	Meer
Sehnsucht	Schnee
Ehre	Klee
Reh	Fee
3. Weg	den
heben	dem
legen	der
ewig	schwer
wer	elend

Exceptions

In a few words, however, *e* is closed before two or more consonants. Memorize these:

1. *e* followed by *r* + consonant:

erst	(first)
Erde	(earth)
Herd	(hearth)
Schwert	(sword)
wert	(worth)
Beschwerde	(complaint)
Pferd	(horse)
werden	(become)

The word *Erz,* meaning metal, ore, is pronounced with [e]. The syllable *Erz-,* meaning arch- (archangel, archbishop, etc.) is pronounced as expected with [ε].

2. e *followed by other consonants:*

stets	(always)
Krebs	(crab, cancer)
Geste	(gesture)

[ε]

Short and open [ε] is approximately the same as the vowel sound in English *best,* but without any of the diphthongal elements typical of some accents in the United States.

Before two or more consonants *e* is usually short and open, as in *Bett* [bεt] (bed).

Exercise 6.21   Pronounce the following words containing [ɛ]:

1. Held	2. stecken	3. Vers
Bett	gelb	Verse
Recht	denn	Herz
Sessel	senden	Herzog
Stelle		fertig

Exceptions

In a few instances, *e* is open before a single consonant. Memorize the following:

1. es   (it)
   des   (of the)
   weg   (away)

   The particle *weg* forms many compounds, e.g. *hinweg, durchweg, weggehen,* in which the vowel is always pronounced [ɛ]. Contrast with the noun *Weg* and its compounds, e.g. *Wegweiser, Heimweg,* in which the vowel is always pronounced [e].

2. The prefixes
   er-   erkennen (recognize)
   ver-   verlieren (lose)
   zer-   zerstören (destroy)

   These are pronounced with open [ɛ] whether they are followed by a vowel or by a consonant.

Exercise 6.22   Differentiate between [e] and [ɛ] in the following pairs:

1. Heer	Herr
2. den	denn
3. wen	wenn
4. Kehle	Kelle
5. legte	leckte
6. zehren	zerren
7. fehl	Fell
8. Beet	Bett

Exercise 6.23   Pronounce the following words, applying the rules for the pronunciation of open and closed vowels:

1. See, Nebel, ewig, essen, schelten, wehen
2. stehlen, Elend, hell, bersten, ersten
3. stets, des, wer, Weh, flehen, Weg
4. geben, weg, es, Herd, Werk, Lerche, lernen
5. Herz, Erzengel, Erde, dem, Epik

Exercise 6.24   Transcribe the above words into the IPA.

Unaccented *e*.

[ə]

Unaccented *e* is traditionally represented in reference works and textbooks as [ə]. In actual practice, singers *regularly* use [ə] only for final *e,* as in *bitte* ['bItə] (please), and *e* in some unaccented middle syllables.

Exercise 6.25 Pronounce the following words containing [ə]:

1. rechte	lege	2. Taugenichts
Stelle	schwere	liebevoll
lasse	stehle	bessere
kämme	Ehre	bittere
hebe		

In all other unaccented syllables, but specifically in the prefixes *ge-* and *be-,* the adjective endings *-es, -en, -em,* and the verb endings *-en, -et, -est,* singers tend to front the vowel somewhat, achieving a quality more akin to [e] or [ɛ] than [ə]. However, since the references use [ə] in transcribing these syllables, this text will also follow this practice except for the syllables described in the next paragraph. The voice student is urged to listen carefully to established singers to determine how much and in what positions [ə] can be fronted.

It is important to note that unaccented *e* is not long and closed if followed by *h* or any other single consonant. Thus *gehangen* (hung) and *gegeben* (given) would be transcribed [gə'haŋən], [gə'gebən].

The prefixes *er-, ver-, zer-, emp-, ent-*

In the prefixes *er-, ver-, zer-, emp-,* and *ent-, e* should always be pronounced and transcribed [ɛ], even though these syllables are almost always unaccented, e.g. *erfahren* [ɛɒ'farən] (experience), *vergessen* [fɛɒ'gɛsən] (forget).

Exercise 6.26 Pronounce the following words paying special attention to the pronunciation of unaccented *e:*

1. gegeben	2. kühles	3. schweben
geehrt	kühlen	schwebest
begraben	kühlem	schwebet
beleben		
geheimer		

Exercise 6.27 Pronounce the following words, paying special attention to the pronunciation of unaccented *e:* .

1. meine, meinen, meinem, Geliebte, Geliebten, begegnen
2. stille, stilles, stillen, Garten, Sammetkleide
3. betend, werde, betreten, geteilt, betete

Exercise 6.28   Transcribe the words in Exercise 6.27 into the IPA.

Excerpts   Read the following excerpts aloud, concentrating on the pronunciation of *e:*

1. Dem Schnee, dem Regen,
Dem Wind entgegen,
Im Dampf der Klüfte,
Durch Nebeldüfte.

> *Rastlose Liebe*
> Schubert

2. Wer trägt der Himmel unzählbare Sterne?
    Wer führt die Sonn' aus ihrem Zelt?
Sie kommt und leuchtet und lacht uns von ferne
    Und läuft den Weg gleich als ein Held.

Kannst du der Wesen unzählbare Heere,
    Den kleinsten Staub fühllos beschaun?
Durch wen ist alles? O gib ihm die Ehre!
    "Mir," ruft der Herr, "sollst du vertraun."

> *Die Ehre Gottes aus der Natur*
> C.P.E. Bach

Song   Sing the following song, paying special attention to all *e*'s, accented
and unaccented.

Guten Abend, gut' Nacht

Gu - ten A - bend, gut' Nacht,   mit__ Ro - sen be -
Gu - ten A - bend, gut' Nacht,   von__ Eng - lein be -

dacht,___ mit___ Näg - lein be - steckt, schlupf un - ter die
wacht,___ die___ zei - gen im___ Traum dir___ Christ - kind - leins

Deck'. Mor - gen früh, wenn Gott will, wirst du wie - der ge -
Baum. Schlaf nun se - lig und süss, schau im Traum's pa - ra -

weckt,___ mor - gen früh, wenn Gott will, wirst du wie - der ge - weckt.
dies,___ schlaf nun se - lig und süss, schau im Traum's pa - ra - dies.

SECTION 4: *ö*

The letter *ö* (also spelled *oe*) represents sounds which are variations of the sounds of *e*.

[ø]

Long and closed [ø] is the same sound as long and closed [e], but pronounced with the lips rounded. Pronounce an extended [e:::::] and, *without changing the position of the tongue or jaw,* slowly round the lips. Be aware that you are really pronouncing the sound [e]. Keep the sides of the tongue against the upper molars and the tip of the tongue against the base of the lower teeth; now, practice alternating [e] and [ø] by slowly rounding and unrounding the lips while pronouncing [e:::::].

The pronunciation of *ö* is regularly long and closed [ø] before *h,* as in *fröhlich* ['frølɪç] (merry), and before a single consonant, as in *schön* [ʃøn] (lovely).

Exercise 6.29	Contrast [e] and [ø] in the following pairs of words:

1.	Meere	Möhre
2.	Lehne	Löhne
3.	lesen	lösen
4.	Besen	bösen
5.	verheeren	verhören
6.	flehe	Flöhe
7.	beten	böten
8.	hebe	höbe
9.	hehlen	Höhlen
10.	sehne	Söhne

Exercise 6.30	Pronounce only the words with *ö* in Exercise 6.29.

Exceptions

There are a few words in which *ö* is pronounced closed before two or more consonants. Memorize these:

1. before *ss* in:
   Grösse   (greatness)
   grösser-, grösst-   (greater, greatest)
   Blösse   (bareness)
   stösst   (pushes)
2. before *st* in:
   trösten   (console)
   rösten   (roast)
3. before *ch* in:
   höchst [høçst]   (highly)

[œ]

Short and open [œ] is the same as short and open [ɛ] but pronounced with the lips rounded. Fix the jaw and tongue for [ɛ] and pronounce an extended [ɛ:::::]; then, *without changing the position of the tongue or jaw,* slowly round the lips, but not as much as for [ø]. Remember that [e] and [ø] are both closed sounds and [ɛ] and [œ] are both open sounds.

Now practice alternating [ɛ] and [œ] by slowly rounding and unrounding the lips while pronouncing [ɛ:::::]. The pronunciation of *ö* is regularly short and open [œ] before two or more consonants, as in *möchte* ['mœçtə] (would like).

Exercise 6.31   Contrast [ɛ] and [œ] in the following pairs of words:

1. Mächte   möchte
2. stecke   Stöcke
3. helle   Hölle
4. Kellner   Kölner
5. fällig   völlig
6. fechte   föchte
7. Schwämme   schwömme
8. kernig   körnig

Exercise 6.32   Pronounce only the words with *ö* in Exercise 6.31.

Exercise 6.33   Contrast the following pairs of words containing [ø] and [œ]:

1. Höhle   Hölle
2. gewöhnen   gewönnen
3. Söhne   sönne
4. Höker   Höcker
5. Schösse   schösse
6. blöken   Blöcken

Exercise 6.34   Pronounce the following words, applying the rules for closed and open monophthongs:

1. versöhnen, böse, möchte, östlich, Getöse
2. öde, Töchter, plötzlich, töten, Schöpfer
3. nötig, Erlkönig, grösste, schön, trösten
4. köstlich, höchstens, Dörflein, Blösse, schösse
5. höher, fröhlich, Löcher, völlig, könnte

Exercise 6.35   Transcribe the above examples into the IPA.

Exercise 6.36   Read the following transcriptions aloud:

1. ['høːrən, 'ʃtønən, 'lœʃən, 'tønə, gœnt]
2. [den, 'edəl, 'løzən, dɛn, 'felɒ, 'lyrɪʃ]

3. [ˈhɛftIçstən, ˈœfnən, ˈløvə, gəˈbet, veɒ]

4. [iˈde, ˈgœtɒ, ˈkœrpɒ, Inˈdem, hInˈvɛk]

5. [ˈplœtslIç, mœnç, bəˈdɑxt, ˈflɛçtən, ˈtøtlIç]

Excerpts

Read the following excerpts aloud, concentrating on the pronunciation of *ö:*

1. Kömmt mir der Tag in die Gedanken,
   Möcht' ich noch einmal rückwärts sehn,
   Möcht' ich zurücke wieder wanken,
   Vor ihrem Hause stille stehn.

   Die Winterreise
   Schubert

2. Will dich im Traum nicht stören,
   Wär' Schad' um deine Ruh',
   Sollst meinen Tritt nicht hören—
   Sacht, sacht die Türe zu!

   Die Winterreise
   Schubert

Tape

Practice speaking the text of the following song. Then read it onto a tape without stopping the recorder.

Song

Sing the following song, concentrating on the pronunciation of *ö.*

Heidenröslein

Hei - den, war so jung und mor - gen - schön, lief er schnell, es
Hei - den!" Rös - lein sprach: "Ich ste - che dich, dass du e - wig
Hei - den, Rös - lein wehr - te sich und stach, half ihm doch__ kein

nah zu sehn, sah's mit vie - len Freu - den. Rös - lein, Rös - lein
denkst an mich und ich wills__ nicht lei - den." Rös - lein, Rös - lein
Weh und Ach, musst es e - ben lei - den. Rös - lein, Rös - lein

Rös - lein rot, Rös - lein auf der Hei - den!
Rös - lein rot, Rös - lein auf der Hei - den!
Rös - lein rot, Rös - lein auf der Hei - den!

SECTION 5: *o*

[o]

Long and closed [o] is similar to the initial element in the English diphthong
[oU], as in *lone* [loUn]. In pronouncing [oU], note how the jaw and the tip
of the tongue rise slightly for the second part of the diphthong.

In articulating the German sound [o], as in *Lohn* [lon] (wage), all movement of the tongue and jaw, and hence all trace of the English diphthongal element [U], must be avoided. First practice pronouncing an extended [o:::::::] allowing no movement of tongue or jaw. Then practice pronouncing *Lohn*, exaggerating the length of the vowel—[lo:::::::n]—and allowing the tip of the tongue to rise only when articulating the [n].

The pronunciation of *o* is regularly long and closed [o] (1) when it occurs in an accented syllable before *h: ohne* ['onə] (without); (2) when it occurs doubled: *Boot* [bot] (boat); and (3) when it occurs before a single consonant: *schon* [ʃon] (already).

Exercise 6.37   Pronounce the following words containing [o]:

1. ohne	2. Boot
Sohle	Moos
Lohn	Moor
froh	
empfohlen	
Kohle	

3. Boden	Hof
holen	Ton
Monat	rot
Vogel	schon
Not	Tor
Los	Tod
	vor

Exceptions

In a number of words, *o* is long and closed before two or more consonants. Memorize these:

1. in *hoch* (high) and its many compounds, for instance,
   hocherfreut
   Hochgefühl
   hochbegabt
   however, *o* is short and open in *Hochzeit* (wedding)!
2. before *st* in:
Ostern	(Easter)
Kloster	(cloister)
prost	(a toast)
Trost	(solace)
getrost	(confident)
3. before *ss* in:
bloss	(bare, simply)
Schoss	(lap)
gross	(large, great)
stossen	(push)

4. also in:

Mond   (moon)
Montag   (Monday)
Obst   (fruit)
Vogt   (warden, governor)

[ɔ]

Short and open [ɔ] is similar to the English sound represented by the same symbol, but it is usually much shorter and slightly more open. It is very much like the *o* sound in the British pronunciation of the word *hot.* Short [ɔ] occurs regularly before two or more consonants, as in *doch* [dɔχ] (but).

Exercise 6.38   Pronounce the following words, using [ɔ] for *o:*

1. hoffen   2. Sommer
   kommen   Sonne
   wollen   Wolke
   fordern   voll
   Sporn   folgen
   Rock   Schopf

3. stolz   4. Frosch
   Stock   Groschen
   Bock   doch
   dort   noch
   fort   Joch
   Holz   Woche

Exceptions

In a few words, *o* is short and open before a single consonant. Memorize these:

1. some words ending in unaccented *-or:*
   Doktor   (doctor)
   Marmor   (marble)
2. also in:
   ob   (whether)
   von, vom   (of, of the)

Exercise 6.39   Contrast [o] and [ɔ] in the following pairs:

1. Gote   Gotte
2. wohne   Wonne
3. Tone   Tonne
4. bog   Bock
5. Wohle   Wolle
6. bohrte   Borte
7. Hofe   hoffe
8. Ofen   offen

Exercise 6.40

Pronounce the following words containing *o,* following the rules for closed and open monophthongs:

1. Vogel, stolz, ohne, drohen, Tonne, mochte
2. Stoff, Mond, gestohlen, Dolch, Sonne, Sohn
3. hoch, Kloster, kosten, Trost, Posten, Ostern, Osten
4. Schoss, schoss, Schloss, grossen, Ross, blosse
5. Horizont, Obst, ob, Ton, von, vom, Dom
6. Hochzeit, Wollust, gestossen, gegossen, Marmor, Gold
7. empor, Bischof, Kleinod, Komik, davon, frohlocken

Exercise 6.41

Transcribe the words in Exercise 6.40 into the IPA.

Excerpts

Read the following excerpts aloud, paying careful attention to the pronunciation of *o:*

1. Als müsste in den Garten,
   Voll Rosen weiss und rot,
   Mein' Liebste auf mich warten,
   Und ist doch lange tot.

   Erinnerung
   Schumann

2. Alles nimmt sie, was nur hold,
   Nimmt das Silber weg des Stromes,
   Nimmt vom Kupferdach des Domes
   Weg das Gold.

   Die Nacht
   Richard Strauss

Song

Sing the following two songs, concentrating on the pronunciation of *o.*

Lili Marleen

Vor der Ka-ser-ne vor dem gro-ssen Tor stand 'ne La-ter-ne und
Uns-re bei-den Schat-ten sah'n wie ei-ner aus; dass wir so lieb uns hat-ten,das
Schon rief der Po-sten:"sie bla-sen Zap-fen-streich, es kann drei Tage ko-sten;"Kam'-
Dei-ne Schritte kennt sie, dei-nen zie-ren Gang, al-le A-bend brennt sie, doch

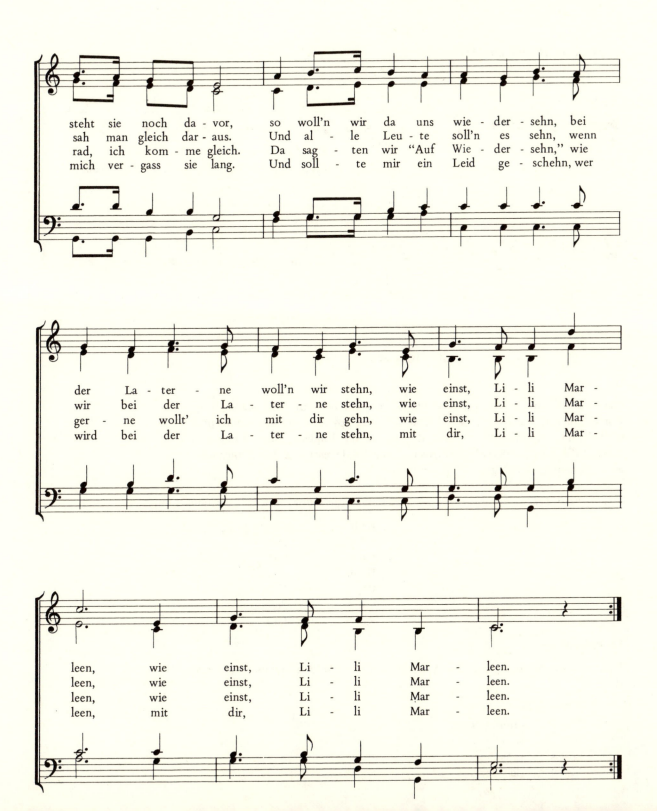

steht sie noch da - vor, so woll'n wir da uns wie - der - sehn, bei
sah man gleich dar - aus. Und al - le Leu - te soll'n es sehn, wenn
rad, ich kom - me gleich. Da sag - ten wir "Auf Wie - der - sehn," wie
mich ver - gass sie lang. Und soll - te mir ein Leid ge - schehn, wer

der La - ter - ne woll'n wir stehn, wie einst, Li - li Mar -
wir bei der La - ter - ne stehn, wie einst, Li - li Mar -
ger - ne wollt' ich mit dir gehn, wie einst, Li - li Mar -
wird bei der La - ter - ne stehn, mit dir, Li - li Mar -

leen, wie einst, Li - li Mar - leen.
leen, wie einst, Li - li Mar - leen.
leen, wie einst, Li - li Mar - leen.
leen, mit dir, Li - li Mar - leen.

O wie wohl ist mir am Abend

(Canon)

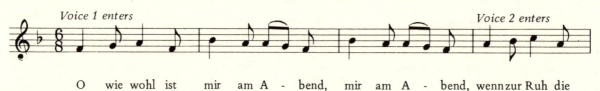

O   wie wohl ist   mir   am A - bend,   mir   am A - bend, wenn zur Ruh die

Glok - ken läu - ten, Glok - ken läu - ten, bim, bam,   bim, bam,   bim, bam!

SECTION 6: *u*

[u]

German long and closed [u] is similar to the English vowel in *moot* [mut].
For German [u], as in *Mut* [mut] (courage), the lips are somewhat more protruded and somewhat more rounded than for the English sound. Long and
closed [u] occurs regularly before *h* as in *Ruhe* ['ruə] (rest) or a single consonant
as in *Mut* [mut] (courage).

Exercise 6.42   Pronounce the following words containing [u]:

1. Kuh	2. rufen
Schuh	gut
Huhn	nun
Buhle	schuf
Uhr	Flug
Stuhl	Schule
Ruhe	Dur

Exceptions

In a number of words, *u* is closed before two or more consonants. Memorize
these:

1. before *ss* in:

Busse	(atonement)
Fuss	(foot)
Gruss	(greeting)
Musse	(leisure)

2. before *ch* in:
    Buch   (book)
    Tuch   (cloth)
    ruchlos   (wicked)
    suchen   (seek)
    Fluch   (curse)
    Kuchen   (cake)
3. before *st* in:
    Schuster   (shoemaker)
    husten   (cough)
4. also in:
    Geburt   (birth)

[U]

German short and open [U] is very similar to the vowel sound in English *puts* [pUts]. It occurs regularly before two or more consonants, as in *muss* [mUs] (must).

Exercise 6.43   Pronounce the following words using [U] for *u:*

1. Putz
   Wunder
   Kunst
   Kupfer
   Busch
2. Schutz
   Luft
   Druck
   nutzen
   bunt
3. Wunsch
   gesund
   Götterfunken
   Puppe
   dumm
4. muss
   Fluss
   Frucht
   Flucht
   wusste

Exceptions

There are a few words in which *u* is open before a single consonant. Memorize the following:

um   (around, also a prefix)
un-   (prefix meaning *un-*)
Rum   (rum)
zum   (to the; but *u* in *zu* is always closed)

Exercise 6.44   Contrast [u] and [U] in the following pairs:

1. Mus   muss
2. Muhme   Mumme
3. schuft   Schuft

4. Ruhm	Rum
5. sucht	Sucht
6. spuken	spucken
7. Stuhle	Stulle
8. Buhle	Bulle
9. bucht	Bucht
10. flucht	Flucht
11. Flugs	flugs

Exercise 6.45

Pronounce the following words containing *u*, applying the rules for closed and open monophthongs:

1. Flut, Mutter, Bube, du, rufen, Kunst
2. Luft, Lust, Puls, Kurs, Kur, Kultur, hundert
3. Umsturz, Bucht, Buch, Kuss, Fluss, Fuss
4. Brusttuch, Schuster, Muster, Demut, Fluch, fluchen
5. Blut, Armut, Bruch, Schuss, lustig, Brust
6. Kutsche, jung, genug, gute, Geduld, Druck
7. Wurzel, bewundern, Mund, Bursche, Genuss

Exercise 6.46

Transcribe the above words into the IPA.

Exercise 6.47

Read the following transcriptions aloud:

1. ['bulə, fluk, zuχt, frUχt, hUlt, juχ'he]
2. [grop, 'honIç, not, 'zɔndɒn, a'pɔstəl, zɔlç]
3. [ɛɒ'lɔʃən, gə'nɔsən, gUnst, fɛɒ'fluχt, 'buzən]

Note: [ʔ] represents a glottal stop (see Chapter 7).

[ze ʔIç zi ʔam baχə 'zItsən
vɛn zi 'fligən‚nɛtsə ʃtrIkt
'odɒ 'zɔntaks fyɒ di 'fɛnstɒ
'frIʃə 'vizən‚blumən pflYkt

ze ʔIç zi tsUm 'gaɾtən 'vandəln
mIt dem 'kœrpçən ʔIn deɒ hant
naχ den 'ɛrstən 'berən 'ʃpɛɒn
an deɒ 'grynən 'dɔrnən‚vant]

Excerpts

Read the following excerpts, paying special attention to the pronunciation of *u:*

1. Herzeleid und viel Verdruss—
   Eine Schul' und enge Mauern,—
   Carreaukönig, der bedauern,
   Und zuletzt mich trösten muss.—
   Ein Geschenk auf art'ge Weise—
   Er entführt mich—Eine Reise—
   Geld und Lust im Überfluss!

   Die Kartenlegerin
   Schumann

2. Und du singst, was ich gesungen,
   Was mir aus der vollen Brust
   Ohne Kunstgepräng' erklungen,
   Nur der Sehnsucht sich bewusst.

   An die ferne Geliebte
   Beethoven

Tape

Practice reading the lyrics of the following song. Then read them onto a tape without stopping the recorder.

Song

Sing the following song, concentrating on the pronunciation of *u.*

Die Lorelei

Ich weiss nicht, was soll es be - deu - ten, dass ich so trau - rig
Die schön - ste Jung - Frau sit - zet dort o - ben wun - der -
Den Schif - fer im klei - nen Schif - fe er - greift es mit wil - dem

bin;_____ ein Mär - chen aus al - ten Zei - ten, das
bar;_____ ihr gol - dnes Ge - schmei - de blit - zet, sie
Weh;_____ er schaut nicht die Fel - sen - rif - fe, er

kommt mir nicht aus dem Sinn._____ Die Luft_____ ist kühl und es
kämmt ihr gol - de - nes Haar._____ Sie kämmt es mit gol - de - nem
schaut nur hin - auf in Höh'._____ Ich glau - be die Wel - len ver -

dun - kelt und ru - hig fliesst_____ der Rhein;_____ der
Kam - me und singt ein Lied_____ da - bei,_____ das
schlin - gen am En - de Schif - fer und Kahn_____ und

Gip - fel des Ber - ges fun - kelt im A - bend-son - nen - schein.____
hat ei - ne Wun - der - sa - me ge - walt' - ge Me - lo - dei.____
das hat mit ih - rem Sin - gen die Lo - re - lei__ ge - tan.____

Chapter 7 | Word Structure

SECTION 1: *STRUCTURAL ELEMENTS*

There are certain problems of pronunciation that can be resolved only through a knowledge of German word structure. These problems require identification of four main types of structural elements: (1) prefixes; (2) suffixes; (3) parts of compound words; (4) inflectional endings. Perhaps surprisingly, the rules for syllable division in simple words do not provide significant information in determining pronunciation.[1]

Prefixes

The following is a list of German prefixes which give rise to problems in pronunciation. You will recall that several prefixes do not conform to the rules of pronunciation; transcriptions of these prefixes are provided.

ab-	abreisen	['ɑpˌrɑezən]	(depart)
an-	ankommen	['anˌkɔmən]	(arrive)
auf-	aufsehen	['aofˌzeən]	(look up)
aus-	ausruhen	['aosˌruən]	(rest)
be- [bə]	beglücken	[bə'glYken]	(make happy)
bei-	Beifall	['baeˌfɑl]	(applause]
da-	dafür	[dɑ'fyɒ]	(for it)
dar-	Darstellung	['darˌʃtɛlUŋ]	(performance)

[1] Although the rules for syllable division in simple words do not provide material help in determining pronunciation, they are outlined here for the singer's information since every musical score contains words that are divided into syllables to be sung on different notes:

1. Division falls before a single consonant: ge-ben, Frie-den. Since *ch, sch,* ß, *ph,* and *th* represent single sounds, the syllable division falls before them: Be-cher, lö-schen, Stra-ße, Te-le-phon, A-po-the-ke.

2. It falls before the final consonant of a cluster: kämp-fen, hol-der, sen-den. The combination *ck* is written *k-k* when divided: blik-ken = blicken.

3. Although in simple words double consonants represent single sounds, they are separated in syllable division: ret-ten, Was-ser, hel-le.

4. The combination *st,* although it represents two sounds, is never separated in simple words: be-ste, Mei-ster.

durch-	durchspielen	['dUrç‚ʃpilən]	(play through)
ein-	einsingen	['aen‚zIŋən]	(practice singing)
ent- [ɛnt]	entlaufen	[ɛnt'laofən]	(run away)
er- [ɛɒ]	erfüllen	[ɛɒ'fYlən]	(fulfill)
fort-	fortlaufen	['fɔrt‚laofən]	(run away)
ge- [gə]	gesehen	[gə'zeən]	(seen)
her-	herkommen	['hɛɒ‚kɔmən]	(come here)
hin- [hIn]	hingehen	['hIn‚geən]	(go there)
miss-	misstrauen	['mIstraoən]	(mistrust)
mit- [mIt]	mitgehen	['mIt‚geən]	(go along)
nach-	nacheilen	['naχ‚ʔaelən]	(hurry after)
über-	überfluten	[ybɒ'flutən]	(overflow)
um- [Um]	Umweg	['Um‚vek]	(detour)
un- [Un]	unglücklich	['Un‚glYklIç]	(unhappy)
unter-	unterirdisch	['Untɒ‚ʔIrdIʃ]	(subterranean)
ur-	uralt	['ur‚ʔalt]	(very old)
ver- [fɛɒ]	vergolden	[fɛɒ'gɔldən]	(gild)
vor-	Vorsicht	['foɒ‚zIçt]	(foresight)
weg- [vɛk]	weggehen	['vɛk‚geən]	(go away)
zer- [tsɛɒ]	zerreissen	[tsɛɒ'raesən]	(tear up)
zu-	zueilen	['tsu‚ʔaelən]	(hurry to)

The pronunciation of each prefix is constant, regardless of what follows it, since a prefix always constitutes a separate structural element in a word. When *her-* is unaccented, as in *hervor* [hɛɒ'foɒ] (forth), it is pronounced [hɛɒ]; when it is accented, as in *herkommen* ['hɛɒkɔmən] (come here) or when it stands alone, it is pronounced [hɛɒ].

Suffixes

The suffixes most likely to affect the pronunciation of a preceding element are:

-bar	trinkbar	['trIŋkbar]	(drinkable)
-chen	Männchen	['mɛnçən]	(little man)
-haft	mannhaft	['manhaft]	(manly)
-heit	Kindheit	['kInthaet]	(childhood)
-keit	Göttlichkeit	['gœtlIçkaet]	(godliness)
-lein	Männlein	['mɛnlaen]	(little man)
-lich	freundlich	['frɔøntlIç]	(friendly)
-los	herzlos	['hɛrtslos]	(heartless)
-nis	Finsternis	['fInstɒnIs]	(darkness)
-sal	Trübsal	['trypzal]	(sorrow)
-sam	wachsam	['vaxzam]	(wakeful)
-schaft	Landschaft	['lantʃaft]	(landscape)
-tum	Reichtum	['raeçtum]	(wealth)

Since the above prefixes and suffixes can have a significant effect on the pronunciation of a word, they should be learned for recognition.

Compound Words

German is well known for its many compound words, such as *Waldeinsamkeit* and *Meistersinger*. In many instances, the singer must be able to break the words into their component elements in order to pronounce them correctly. Some words are simply put together, like *Meistersinger.* Others are joined with a connective element. It is helpful to be able to recognize the four common connective elements: (1) *e,* as in *Hundehaus;* (2) *(e)n,* as in *Rosenblatt;* (3) *er,* as in *Kindergarten;* (4) *(e)s,* as in *Liebestraum.* Fortunately, it is usually apparent how compounds should be divided; however, for some words, a knowledge of German is necessary in order to decide pronunciation questions such as unvoicing or division of consonant clusters.

Inflectional Endings

A knowledge of inflection, especially verb inflection, is frequently necessary in order to resolve questions concerning pronunciation.

Below are presented parts of a model verb, *legen,* (to lay), which will be used to illustrate certain pronunciation problems:

Present tense:

ich lege	(I lay, etc.)	wir legen
du legst		ihr legt
er, sie, es legt		sie legen

Past tense:

ich legte	(I laid, etc.)	wir legten
du legtest		ihr legtet
er, sie, es legte		sie legten

Past participle:
gelegt   (laid) (as in *I have laid,* etc.)

Another ending which the student should be able to recognize is the genitive singular *s* of nouns, as in *Betrugs,* genitive of *Betrug* (betrayal).

SECTION 2: PRONUNCIATION PROBLEMS

There are four main types of pronunciation problems that may require a knowledge of the preceding structural elements: (1) vowel quality; (2) unvoicing; (3) division of consonant clusters; (4) use of the glottal stop.

Vowel Quality

In Chapter 6, it was pointed out that a vowel followed by a single consonant is usually closed. In compounds and inflected forms, vowels which are *apparently* followed by two or more consonants are often closed. The words must be broken down into structural elements to determine whether the vowel is in fact followed by a single consonant or more than one consonant.

Prefixes

In general, the pronunciation of a prefix remains the same, regardless of what follows it. Thus the vowel in *vor-* is closed whether it is followed by a vowel or a consonant: *Voreltern* ['foɒˀɛltɒn] (ancestors), *Vorvater* ['foɒfɑtɒ] (fore-father).

A number of prefixes are pronounced with an open vowel even though they end with a single consonant (see list above and Chapter 6); this open pronunciation is not affected by what follows the prefix. Thus the vowel in *mit* is open whether it is followed by a vowel or a consonant: *mitessen* ['mIt-ɛsən] (dine with), *mitgehen* ['mItgeən] (go along).

Suffixes

If a single consonant stands between a vowel and a suffix, as in *Rös-lein,* then the vowel is closed: ['røslɑen].

Exercise 7.1   Pronounce the following words:

1. lesbar	7. tonlos
2. Blümchen	8. Verlöbnis
3. boshaft	9. Trübsal
4. Bosheit	10. strebsam
5. Röslein	11. Botschaft
6. tödlich	

Compounds

If a compound divides so that a vowel is followed by a single consonant as in *Betbuch* (prayer book), then the vowel is closed: ['bet̩buχ].

Exercise 7.2   Pronounce the following compounds:

1. Bluttat	10. jedweder
2. demselben	11. Rotkäppchen
3. Flughafen	12. totschlagen
4. Lebtag	13. Fluggast
5. Lobgesang	14. Guttat
6. Blutgeld	15. Betstunde
7. losgebe	16. Brother
8. fürwahr	17. Wegweiser
9. Hofleute	18. Tonkunst

Inflectional Endings

If a verb has a closed vowel in the infinitive, then this vowel will normally be pronounced closed regardless of inflectional endings:

infinitive: legen ['legən]
present tense: du legst [lekst]
er legt [lekt]
etc.
past tense: ich legte ['lektə]
etc.
past participle: gelegt [gə'lekt]

Likewise, if a noun has a closed vowel, the presence of an inflectional ending will not affect the quality of the vowel:

nominative: Betrug [bə'truk]
genitive: Betrugs [bə'truks]

Words ending in *-er, -el,* and *-en* often lose the *e* when adding inflectional endings or suffixes. This does not affect the quality of a preceding vowel (see also next section).

edel ['edəl]   —   edle ['edlə]
Ekel ['ekəl]   —   eklig ['eklIç]
wider ['vidɒ]   —   widrig ['vidɾIç]

Exercise 7.3   Pronounce the following words containing inflectional endings:

1. lebst
2. bewegt
3. verlobt
4. klebt
5. Bahnhofs
6. verflucht
7. beschwört
8. beschert
9. gegrüsst
10. getönt
11. betont
12. Berufs
13. tobst
14. gelöst
15. grünst
16. büsste
17. hegte
18. lebtest

Unvoicing

The consonants *b, d, g,* and *s*[2] are pronounced as their voiceless equivalents [p, t, k, s] when they occur: (1) at the end of a word, as in *Bad* [bɑt] (bath); (2) before a consonant, as in *Magd* [mɑkt] (maid); (3) at the end of an element in a compound, as in *Abendessen* ['ɑbən t ʔɛsən] (supper).

---

[2] *V* is also affected to some extent by these rules (see Chapter 16), *w* only rarely.

Exercise 7.4 Pronounce the following words:
Tag
Bad
Mond
leb'
Vogt
Abt
beredt

Prefixes

The only important prefix ending in one of these consonants is *ab-*. It is always pronounced [ɑp], as in *abändern* ['ɑpˌʔɛndɒn] (transform), *ablegen* ['ɑpˌlegən] (take off). The singer is cautioned about words such as *aber* ['ɑbɒ] (but) and *Abend* ['ɑbənt] (evening), in which *ab* is not a prefix.

Exercise 7.5 Pronounce the following words:

ablegen
abspielen
abgeneigt
aberkennen
Aberglaube
Abendmahl

Suffixes

Since a number of suffixes begin with consonants, *b, d, g,* and *s* will be unvoiced before them, as, for example, in *freundlich, endlos, Wildnis, strebsam,* and *lesbar.* However, this does not really represent a special case of the general rule, which states simply that *b, d, g,* and *s* are unvoiced before consonants.

When *b, d, g,* or *s* occur before *n, l,* and *r* in inflected forms and derivatives of words ending in *-en, -el, -er,* they are *not* usually unvoiced. It will not always be easy for the singer with only a passing knowledge of German to recognize such forms. A number of examples are listed in the exercise below to provide some familiarity with the type. Recall from the previous section that closed vowels remain closed in such inflected forms and derivatives as *edle* ['edlə], *ebne* ['ebnə].

Exercise 7.6 Pronounce the following words paying special attention to *b, d, g,* and *s:*

1. siedle (< siedeln)
2. Siedlung (< siedeln)
3. edle (< edel)
4. Adlige (< Adel)
5. Adler (< Adel)
6. ebne (< eben)

13. Wandrer (< wandern)
14. Wagner (< Wagen)
15. Wandlung (< wandeln)
16. Bogner (< Bogen)
17. regnet (< Regen)
18. irdne (< irden)

7. übler (< übel)

8. goldne (< golden)

9. handle (< handeln)

10. eigner (< eigen)

11. andre (< ander)

12. seidnes (< seiden)

19. Redner (< reden)

20. Ordnung (< older form *or-denung*)

21. unsre (< unser)

22. heisrem (< heiser)

23. Gegner (< gegen)

24. Lügner (< lügen)

Compounds

If an element in a compound ends in *b, d, g,* or *s* and is followed by an element beginning with a consonant, as in *Mondschein* (moonlight), *Diebstahl* (theft), the voiced consonant is of course unvoiced: ['mont,ʃaen, 'dip,ʃtɑl].

The singer does not really have to be able to separate the elements, since *b, d, g,* and *s* are unvoiced before any consonant. If, however, the second element begins with a vowel, the singer must be able to break down the word in order to know that the consonant is at the end of the first element and unvoiced rather than at the beginning of the second element and voiced. In *Lesart* ['les,ɑrt] (version) and *Blasinstrument* ['blɑsʔInstru,mɛnt] (wind instrument), for example, it is important to recognize that *s* belongs to the first element and is pronounced [s]; if it belonged to the second element, it would be pronounced [z].

Exercise 7.7   Pronounce the following words:

1. Werbgesang
2. Abendsonne
3. bergab
4. bergauf
5. endgültig
6. Argwohn
7. Abendessen
8. bandartig
9. Bergsteiger
10. Bildhauer

Inflection

If a voiced consonant appears before an ending beginning with a consonant, then of course it becomes unvoiced: *legst* [lekst], *legt* [lekt], *gelegt* [gə'lekt], *Betrugs* [bə'truks].

Consonant Clusters

Certain combinations of consonants have a special pronunciation when they appear together in a simple word. If, however, the same consonants appear together but belong to different elements in a compound, they must be pronounced, not as a unit, but as parts of the separate elements.

For example, *sch* is pronounced [ʃ] in a simple word such as *löschen* ['lœʃən] (extinguish). If, however, *s* and *ch* come together as parts of two different elements, as they do in *Röschen* (little rose), then this must be reflected in the pronunciation: ['røsçən].

Double consonants are usually pronounced the same as single consonants in simple words, as *tt* in *Betten* ['bɛtən] (beds). If, on the other hand, the double consonant represents parts of two elements, as *tt* in *Bettag* (day of prayer), the length of the *t* is doubled: ['bet,tɑk].

The combinations *bl, br, gl, gr, dr, pl, pr, kl, kr, tr, fr, fl, schr, schl, schm,* and *schn* are also pronounced as units in simple words. If, however, part of such a combination belongs to one element and part to another, each part of the combination is pronounced with its respective element rather than as a unit. Contrast for example *zugleich (zu + gleich)* (together), pronounced [tsu'glɑeç], and *Zugluft (Zug + luft)* (draft), pronounced ['tsuk,lUft]. The difference is in some instances more striking in singing than in speaking. A combination such as *bl, kr,* or *fl* will be launched on one note if it belongs to one element; if, however, the combination is composed of parts of two elements, the first part will be sung on one note, the second on the next.

Prefixes

Since a number of the prefixes end in consonants, a variety of consonant combinations occur in words containing prefixes. The prefix always constitutes a separate element, and its final consonant should not be carried over to the next element.

Exercise 7.8

(1) Pronounce the following words; (2) transcribe them into the IPA; (3) indicate how the consonant clusters in each word would be divided between notes by drawing a line between the sounds, for example, *zugleich* [tsu|'glɑeç].

1. abrenne, abbrennen, angehen, Vorrat, Verrat
2. entrüstet, unnötig, fortrennen, herritt, Hinnahme

Suffixes

The initial consonant of a suffix together with the final consonant of the preceding element may form a problem cluster. Like a prefix, a suffix always constitutes a separate element and its initial consonant should be pronounced separately from the preceding consonant, as in *lieblich* ['lip|lIç] (lovable).

Exercise 7.9

Follow the instructions for Exercise 7.8.

glaublich
endlich
sorglos
Derbheit
verschiebbar

Compounds

In compounds also, problem clusters may be formed at the junction of two elements. Here, too, each element is pronounced separately and consonant sounds are not blended across the boundary, for example, *Zugluft* ['tsuk|ˌlUft].

The final consonants of the connecting elements *(e)s, er,* and *(e)n* will always be separated from following consonants, as in *Todestag* ['todəs|tɑk] (day of death).

Exercise 7.10	Follow the instructions for Exercise 7.8.

      1. arglistig, Arbeitstisch, Betstunde, Dankrede

      2. Donnerstag, Festrede, huldreich, Bergland

Inflection

Problem clusters are not generally formed by the addition of inflectional endings.

It should be clear from the foregoing that a fair knowledge of German is necessary to divide some problem clusters. The novice cannot really be expected to know how to divide *Zugluft* or *zugleich.* Or consider the unusual form *erblich.* As a verb meaning "grew pale," it is divided into the prefix *er-* and the root *blich* and is pronounced [ɛɒ|'blIç]. As an adjective meaning "hereditary," it is divided into the root *erb-* and the suffix *-lich* and is pronounced ['ɛɾp|lIç]. However, the singer should at least learn to recognize the problem situations and will probably develop a fair intuition about dividing consonant clusters as they are treated individually in greater detail in the following sections on consonants.

Glottal Stop [ʔ]

The glottal stop, indicated by the symbol [ʔ], is the brief stoppage of air before articulating a following sound, usually a vowel. It can prevent *an aim* [ən ʔeIm] from sounding like *a name* [ə neIm]. In some areas, especially around New York City, this sound is substituted for *t* in words like *bottle* ['bɑʔl].

In German, almost every word beginning with a vowel is preceded by a glottal stop. This is just the reverse of French, in which glottal stops are avoided and a final consonant in one word is carried over to a following word beginning with a vowel.

Exercise 7.11	Practice separating with a glottal stop the words beginning with a vowel in the following phrases:

      1. die alte Amme

      2. der erste Akt

      3. ein altes Erbe

The glottal stop is used not only at the beginning of words; it is regularly used in certain positions within words.

Prefixes

As we have pointed out, any prefix constitutes a separate element and should be pronounced as a unit. This means that if the prefix is followed by a vowel, the vowel will usually be preceded by a glottal stop, as in *erinnern* [ɛɒˈʔInɒn] (remember), *beachten* [bəˈʔɑxtən] (take heed).

The prefixes *her-, hin-, dar-,* and *vor-* represent a special case. When they are combined with another prefix beginning with a vowel, there is no glottal stop and the final consonant is drawn to the following syllable, as in *heran* [hɛˈrɑn] (hither), *hinan* [hIˈnɑn] (upward), *daran* [dɑˈrɑn] (to it), and *voran* [foˈrɑn] (forward). However, when they appear before an element other than another prefix, they are pronounced as a unit and followed by a glottal stop if the element begins with a vowel, as in *Vorahnung* [ˈfoɒˌʔɑnUŋ] (premonition). As a general rule, of these four prefixes only *vor* will appear before an element which begins with a vowel but is not a prefix.

Exercise 7.12   Pronounce the following words, using a glottal stop where appropriate:

1. abändern, beobachten, aneignen, auferstehen, fortan
2. ausatmen, einatmen, entarten, erinnern, überantwortet
3. geahnt, geehrt, vereint, Mitarbeiter, unterirdisch
4. nachahmen, überall, vorangehen, vorauseilen, Vorort
5. daraus, missachten, herannahen, uralt, unendlich
6. beiordnen, beirren, durchirren, wegessen, umändern
7. hineingehen, zuerst, forteilen, verteilen, Vorahnung

Exercise 7.13   Transcribe the words in Exercise 7.12 into the IPA. Be sure to note glottal stop with [ʔ].

Suffixes

A suffix will not ordinarily be separated from a preceding element by a glottal stop. For example, in *Ahnung* [ˈɑnUŋ] (notion), the suffix *-ung* is not preceded by a glottal stop.

Compounds

In a compound word, an element that begins with a vowel will normally be preceded by a glottal stop, as in *bergab* [bɛrkˈʔɑp] (downhill). It will require a fair amount of experience and some knowledge of German to recognize how to divide some words.

Exercise 7.14   Pronounce the following words, using a glottal stop where necessary:

1. bergauf, jahrein, kläräugig, herzergreifend, Hufeisen
2. Todesahnung, liebentflammten, Blutacker, Klageruf
3. gottergeben, Götterfunken, Donnerschlag, herzerschütternd, jahraus
4. Liebeserklärung, Meisterehre, Abendessen, unterdessen, Aberglaube
5. bandartig, Blasinstrument, bösartig, Drehorgel, Dreieck
6. ehrerbietig, Handarbeit, Lesart, Tonart

Inflection

An inflectional ending will not normally be separated from a preceding element by a glottal stop; for example, in *bebest* ['bebəst], there is no glottal stop before the ending *-est*.

Excerpts   Read the following excerpts aloud, paying careful attention to the use of glottal stop:

1. ihrem Aug eilt Amor zu

   An Silvia
   Schubert

2. Geuss nicht so laut der liebentflammten Lieder
   Tonreichen Schall
   Vom Blütenast des Apfelbaums hernieder,
   O Nachtigall!

   An die Nachtigall
   Brahms

3. Ich sass zu deinen Füssen in Waldeseinsamkeit;
   Windesatmen, Sehnen ging durch die Wipfel breit.
   In stummen Ringen senkt' ich das Haupt in deinen Schoss,
   und meine bebenden Hände um deine Knie ich schloss.
   Die Sonne ging hinunter, der Tag verglühte all,
   ferne, sang eine Nachtigall, sang eine Nachtigall.

   In Waldeseinsamkeit
   Brahms

Chapter 8 | The Sounds of *b, d, g*

The consonants *b, d, g,* and *s* (see Chapter 10 for *s*) are voiced when they stand before a vowel which is in the same element. You will recall from the previous chapter that when these consonants occur before a consonant, at the end of a word, or at the end of an element in a compound, they become unvoiced. You will also recall that when they appear before *l, n,* or *r* in inflected forms and derivatives of words ending in *-el, -en,* or *-er,* they are not usually unvoiced.

A double consonant in the same element usually follows the same rules for pronunciation as a single consonant, although some feel that it should be somewhat longer in duration.

SECTION 1: *b*

[b]

When followed in the same element by a vowel, *l,* or *r,* the letter *b* is pronounced [b], as in *Eber* ['ebɒ] (boar), *geblickt* [gə'blIkt] (glimpsed), *verbracht* [fɛɒ'brɑχt] (spent). Before *l, n,* or *r* in an inflected form or derivative of a word ending in *-el, -en,* or *-er, b* is considered part of the same element and is pronounced [b], as in *übler* ['yblɒ] (< *übel*) (evil).

[p]

When *b* appears before a consonant, at the end of a word, or at the end of an element, it is pronounced [p]: *Liebster* [lipstɒ] (dearest), *Grab* [grɑp] (grave), *abändern* ['ap͵ʔɛndɒn] (transform), *lieblich* ['liplIç] (dear), *abreisen* ['ap͵rɑezən] (depart).

Exercise 8.1

Contrast voiced and unvoiced *b* in the following pairs of related words:

1. lebe   lebt
2. grabe   gräbst
3. geben   gibt
4. halber   Halbinsel
5. leben   leblos
6. lieben   liebäugeln

bb

Simple Words

In the few words in which *bb* occurs within the same element, it is pronounced according to the rules for *b*, for example, *Ebbe* ['ɛbə] (ebb), *verebbt* [fɛɒ'ʔɛpt] (ebbed).

Compounds

In most instances *bb* occurs at the junction of two elements in a compound, in which case it is pronounced [pb], as in *abbauen* ['ɑp,bɑoən] (dismantle).

Exercise 8.2　　　　Pronounce the following words, paying careful attention to the pronunciation of *b:*

1. bitte, ob, obwohl, lobe, lobt, Lob
2. liebe, lieb, lieblich, geliebt, lieber, Liebchen, Liebschaft
3. schwebt, gibst, trübt, lebst, Leben, grubst
4. Obst, tobt, bebt, übt, Trieb, Triebe
5. Erlebnis, Trübsal, strebsam, leblos, lebhaft
6. abrennen, abbrennen, herabsehen, hinabeilen
7. vergebe, vergeblichen, geblichen, geblasen, gebt, unablässig
8. ablassen, abblassen, erblassen, gebet, Gebet, Verlöbnis
9. Himbeere, aberkennen, Aberglaube, Abende, Schreibpapier
10. grabe, Grab, Grabrede, Krabbe, Ebne, biblisch

Exercise 8.3　　　　Transcribe the words in Exercise 8.2 into the IPA and draw lines through the transcriptions to indicate where a division between notes would fall.

Tape　　　　Make a tape of the following song text, without stopping the recorder:

Du meine Seele, du mein Herz,
Du meine Wonne, du mein Schmerz,
Du meine Welt, in der ich lebe,
Mein Himmel, du, darein ich schwebe,
O du mein Grab, in das hinab
Ich ewig meinen Kummer gab!
Du bist die Ruh, du bist der Frieden,
Du bist der Himmel mir beschieden,
Dass du mich liebst, macht mich mir wert,
Dein Blick hat mich vor mir verklärt,
Du hebst mich liebend über mich,
Mein guter Geist, mein bessres Ich!

Widmung
Schumann

Song   Sing the following song, paying special attention to the pronunciation of *b*.

Ach, wie ist's möglich dann

Ach, wie ist's mög - lich dann, dass ich dich las - sen kann!
Blau ist ein Blü - me - lein, das heisst Ver - giss - nicht - mein.
Wär ich ein Vö - ge - lein, wollt ich bald bei dir sein,

Hab' dich von Her - zen lieb, das glau - be mir!
Dies Blüm - lein leg' ans Herz und denk an mich!
scheut' Falk' und Ha - bicht nicht, flög' schnell zu dir.

Du hast die See - le mein so ganz ge - nom - men ein,
Stirbt Blüt und Hoff - nung gleich, wir sind an Lie - be reich;
Schöss' mich ein Jä - ger tot, fiel' ich in dei - nen Schoss;

dass   ich   kein'   an - dre   lieb   als   dich   al -   lein.
denn   die   stirbt   nie   bei   mir,   das   glau - be   mir!
sähst   du   mich   trau - rig   an,   gern   stürb' ich   dann.

SECTION 2: *d*

[d]

When followed in the same element by a vowel or *r,* the letter *d* is pronounced [d], as in *Ader* ['ɑdɒ] (artery), *bedrohen* [bə'droən] (threaten).

Before *l, n,* or *r* in an inflected form or derivative of a word ending in *-el, -en,* or *-er, d* is considered part of the same element and is pronounced [d], as in *edler* ['edlɒ] (< edel) (noble).

[t]

When *d* appears before a consonant, at the end of a word, or at the end of an element, it is pronounced [t], as in *freundlich* ['frɔøntlIç] (friendly), *Freund* [frɔønt] (friend), *fremdartig* ['frɛmt,ˀɑrtIç] (strange).

Exercise 8.4   Contrast voiced and unvoiced *d* in the following pairs of related words:

1. Lieder   Lied
2. Ende   Endergebnis
3. laden   lädst
4. Stunde   stündlich
5. Kinder   Kind
6. Erde   Erdball

dt

[t]

When the combination *dt* appears within one element, it is pronounced [t], as in *Städte* ['ʃtɛtə] (cities).

[tt]

If *dt* represents parts of two different elements, then it is pronounced [tt], as in *Handtuch* ['hɑntˌtuχ] (towel).

dd

Simple Words

In the handful of words in which *dd* occurs within the same element, it is pronounced according to the rules for *d,* as in *Widder* ['vIdɒ] (ram).

Compounds

Usually, *dd* represents parts of two elements and is pronounced [td], as in *Raddampfer* ['rɑtˌdɑmpfɒ] (paddle steamer).

Exercise 8.5

Pronounce the following words according to the rules for pronunciation of *d:*

1. Dame, bedacht, Feder, Verdruss, endlich, lädt
2. Band, Bande, bandartig, Bandreif, Todesbanden
3. Wildnis, endlos, Feindschaft, Mädchen, widmen, widrig
4. Waldhüter, Lindrung, Geld, seidnes, Waldeinsamkeit
5. tödlich, redlich, Redner, redselig, beredsam, golden, Gold, goldne
6. südlich, sündhaft, Abenddämmerung, verheddern
7. Erde, irdisch, Erdteil, Erdreiste, huldreichstes, Handarbeit
8. Abendröte, Abendstern, Abendessen, anordnen

Excerpts

Read the following excerpts aloud:

1. Was vermeid ich denn die Wege,
   wo die andern Wandrer gehn . . .

   Der Wegweiser
   Schubert

2. Im Felde schleich ich still und wild,
   gespannt mein Feuerrohr,
   da schwebt so licht dein liebes Bild,
   dein süsses Bild mir vor.

   Du wandelst jetzt wohl still und mild
   durch Feld und liebes Thal,
   und, ach, mein schnell verrauschend Bild
   stellt sich dir's nicht einmal?

Mir ist es, denk ich nur an dich,
als in den Mond zu sehn,
ein stiller Friede kommt auf mich,
weiss nicht, wie mir geschehn.

Jägers Abendlied
Schubert

3. Ich hatt' ihn ausgeträumet,
Der Kindheit friedlich schönen Traum,
Ich fand allein mich, verloren
Im öden, unendlichen Raum.

Frauenliebe und Leben
Schumann

Song

Sing the following song, concentrating on the pronunciation of *d*.

Gold und Silber

Gold und Sil - ber lieb ich sehr, könnt' es auch ge - brau - chen;
Seht, wie blinkt der gold - ne Wein hier in mei - nem Be - cher;
Doch viel schö - ner ist das Gold, das vom Lock - en - köpf - chen

hätt ich nur ein gan - zes Meer, mich hin - ein - zu - tau - chen.
hört, wie klin - gen sil - ber - hell Lie - der fro - her Ze - cher.
mei - nes trau - ten Lieb - chens rollt in zwei blon - den Zöpf - chen.

's braucht ja nicht ge - prägt zu sein, hab es sonst auch ger - ne
Dass die Zeit einst gol - den war, möcht ich nicht be - strei - ten,
Dar - um fröh - lich, lie - bes Kind, lass uns her - zen, küs - sen,

gleich des Mon - des Sil - ber - schein und der gold - nen Ster - ne,
denkt man doch im Sil - ber - haar gern ver - gang - ner Zei - ten,
bis die Lok - ken sil - bern sind und wir schei - den müs - sen,

gleich des Mon - des Sil - ber - schein und der gold - nen Ster - ne.
denkt man doch im Sil - ber - haar gern ver - gang - ner Zei - ten.
bis die Lok - ken sil - bern sind und wir schei - den müs - sen.

SECTION 3: *g*

[g]

When followed in the same element by a vowel, *l*, or *r*, the letter *g* is pronounced [g], as in *klagen* ['klɑgən] (lament), *beglücken* [bə'glYkən] (make happy), *begrüssen* [bə'grYsən] (greet).

Before *l*, *n*, or *r* in an inflected form or derivative of a word ending in *-el*, *-en*, or *-er*, *g* is considered part of the same element and is pronounced [g], as in *eigner* ['ɑegnɒ] (own).

[k]

When *g* appears before a consonant, at the end of a word, or at the end of an element, it is pronounced [k], as in *klagt* [klɑkt] (laments), *lag* [lɑk] (lay), *bergab* [bɛrk'ʔɑp] (downhill).

[ʒ]

In a few words of French origin, *g* is pronounced [ʒ]. Memorize the following:

Genie	[ʒe'ni]	(genius)
genieren	[ʒe'nirən]	(embarrass)
Gendarm	[ʒɑn'dɑrm]	(gendarm)
Rage	['rɑʒə]	(rage)
Regie	[re'ʒi]	(direction) (theat.)
Regisseur	[reʒi'søɒ]	(director)
Courage	[ku'rɑʒə]	(courage)
arrangieren	[ɑrã'ʒirən]	(arrange)

Exercise 8.6 Contrast voiced and unvoiced *g* in the following pairs of related words:

1. lagen   lagst
2. bewegen   bewegt
3. Zuge   Zugabteil
4. mögen   möglich
5. Zeuge   Zeugnis
6. hege   hegt

ig

[Iç]

At the end of a word or before a consonant, *-ig* is pronounced [Iç], as in *heilig* ['hɑelIç] (holy), *heiligt* ['hɑelIçt] (consecrates).

[Ig]

Before a vowel, *-ig* is pronounced [Ig], as in *heilige* ['haelIgə] (holy).

[Ik]

Before a syllable ending in the sound [ç] (usually the suffix *-lich*), *-ig* is pronounced [Ik], as in *königlich* ['kønIklIç] (royal).

Exercise 8.7   Contrast the pronunciation of *-ig* in the following pairs of related words:

1. wichtigen   wichtig
2. lockige   lockig
3. beleidigen   beleidigt
4. ewige   Ewigkeit
5. brünstige   brünstigsten
6. wenige   wenigstens

gn

[gn]

If the combination *gn* appears within one element, it is pronounced [gn], as in *Gnom* [gnom] (gnome).

gg

Simple Words

In the few words in which *gg* occurs within the same element, it is pronounced according to the rules for *g*, as in *Flagge* ['flagə] (flag).

Compounds

In most instances, *gg* represents parts of two elements and is pronounced [kg], as in *weggehen* ['vɛk,geən] (go away).

Exercise 8.8   Pronounce the following words, using the rules for pronunciation of *g*:

1. lege, legst, gelegt, Belegs, legte, begleiten
2. Berg, Bergland, Berggeist, Roggen, weggetan
3. Flug, Flugs, Fluggast, flügge, zugleich, Zugluft
4. innig, innige, inniglich, Genie, General, möglich

5. eigen, geeignet, begegnen, behaglich, wenigstens
6. arg, arglos, regnet, Zögling, zogst, Betrugs
7. vergnügt, Traurigkeit, segnen, brünstigsten, Bergnymphe
8. holdseliglich, kreuzigte, Heiligtum, Königreich, bergauf
9. arglistig, jeglich, geglichen, gehegt, Gnade, Gegner
10. vergnügen, wonniglich, fügte, bewogst, heilges, sorglos

Exercise 8.9

Transcribe the words in Exercise 8.8 into the IPA and draw lines through the transcriptions to indicate where divisions between notes would fall.

Excerpts

Read the following excerpts aloud:

1. Es grünet ein Nussbaum vor dem Haus,
   Duftig,
   Luftig
   Breitet er blättrig die Äste aus.

   Der Nussbaum
   Schumann

2. Der Mond scheint hell, der Rasen grün
   ist gut zu unsrem Begegnen,
   du trägst ein Schwert und nickst so kühn,
   Dein Liebschaft will ich segnen, ja segnen!
   Und als erschien der lichte Tag,
   dein Liebschaft will ich segnen, ja segnen!

   Verrat
   Brahms

3. Als ich befriedigt, freudigen Herzens,
   sonst dem Geliebten im Arme lag,
   immer noch rief er, Sehnsucht im Herzen,
   ungeduldig den heutigen Tag.
   Helft mir, ihr Schwestern, helft mir verscheuchen
   eine thörichte Bangigkeit,
   dass ich mit klarem Aug' ihn empfange,
   ihn, die Quelle der Freudigkeit.

   Helft mir, ihr Schwestern
   Schumann

4. Durchzückt von seligsten Genusses Schmerz,
   des heiligsten Blutes Quell
   fühl' ich sich giessen in mein Herz:
   des eignen sündigen Blutes Gewell'.

Parsifal, Act I
Wagner

Song

Sing the following song, paying special attention to the pronunciation
of *g.*

Ich hatt' einen Kameraden

Ich hatt ei - nen Ka - me - ra - den, ei - nen bes - sern findst du
Eine Ku - gel kam ge - flo - gen, gilt sie mir oder gilt sie
Will mir die Hand noch rei - chen, der - weil ich e - ben

nit. Die ___ Trom - mel schlug zum Strei - te, er ___
dir? Ihn ___ hat es weg - ge - ris - sen, er ___
lad: "Kann ___ dir die Hand nicht ge - ben, bleib ___

ging   an   mei - ner   Sei - te   in   glei - chem Schritt und __
liegt   mir   vor   den   Fü - ssen, als   wärs   ein   Stück von __
du   im   ew - gen   Le - ben   mein   gu - ter   Ka - me -

Tritt,   in   glei - chem Schritt   und __   Tritt.
mir,   als   wärs   ein   Stück   von __   mir.
rad,   mein   gu - ter   Ka - me - rad.

Chapter 9 | The Sounds of a, ä, ie

SECTION 1: *a*

Speaking: [a], [ɑ]

In speaking, some distinction in quality is made between long *a* (also spelled *aa*) and short *a* in German. Short *a* is the front vowel [a], found in the English diphthong [aI], as in *ice* [aIs]. Long *a* is the back vowel [ɑ], more nearly akin to the pronunciation of *a* in *father* ['fɑðər].

Singing: [ɑ]

In singing, this differentiation is not customarily made. Also, it is not usually reflected in transcriptions in the standard references. Therefore, the single symbol [ɑ] is used in this text for *a* and *aa*. This convention will furthermore spare you the chore of learning exceptions, of which there are quite a few.

The English-speaking singer should be especially careful about the pronunciation of *a* in unaccented syllables. Although the pronunciation of unaccented *a* is reduced to [ə] in English, as in *America* [ə'mɛrIkə], in German the pronunciation [ɑ] is maintained, as in *Amerika* [ɑ'merIkɑ]. The unaccented prefix *da-*, as in *dafür* [dɑ'fyɒ], tends to be particularly troublesome for English-speaking people.

Exercise 9.1   Pronounce the following words containing unaccented *a*:

Schumann
Telemann
Richard
Judas
dabei

Exercise 9.2   Pronounce the following words, using [ɑ] for *a* in all positions:

1. Dach, Farbe, Kamera, davon, Atlas
2. Saal, Mahl, lassen, Mann
3. Firmament, Afrika, Drama, Anna, allein
4. Amadeus, Akademie, darum, langsam
5. Alabaster, Affekt, Banane, Europa, alleluja

Excerpts

Read the following excerpts aloud:

1. Nun hast du mir den ersten Schmerz getan,
   Der aber traf.
   Du schläfst, du harter, unbarmherz'ger Mann,
   Den Todesschlaf.

   > *Frauenliebe und Leben*
   > Schumann

2. Um Mitternacht hab' ich gedacht
   hinaus in dunkle Schranken.
   Es hat kein Lichtgedanken
   mir Trost gebracht um Mitternacht.

   > *Um Mitternacht*
   > Mahler

3. Ich unglücksel'ger Atlas!
   Eine Welt, die ganze Welt der Schmerzen,
   muss ich tragen,
   ich trage Unerträgliches . . .

   > *Der Atlas*
   > Schubert

4. Allein und abgetrennt von aller Freude,
   seh ich ans Firmament nach jener Seite.

   > *Lied der Mignon*
   > Schubert

Song

Sing the following song, concentrating on the pronunciation of *a*.

Wanderschaft

Das Wan - dern ist des Mül - lers Lust, das Wan - dern ist des
Vom Was - ser ha - ben wir's ge - lernt, vom Was - ser ha - ben
Das sehn wir auch den Rä - dern ab, das sehn wir auch den
O Wan - dern, Wan - dern mei - ne Lust, o Wan - dern, Wan - dern

Müllers Lust, das Wandern!

Mül - lers Lust, das Wan - dern! Das muss ein schlech - ter
wir's ge - lernt, vom Was - ser! Das hat nicht Ruh bei
Rä - dern ab, den Rä - dern! Die gar nicht ger - ne
mei - ne Lust, o Wan - dern! Herr Mei - ster und Frau

Mül - ler sein, dem nie - mals fiel das Wan - dern ein, dem
Tag und Nacht, ist stets auf Wan - der - schaft be - dacht, ist
stil - le stehn und sich bei Tag nicht mü - de drehn, und
Mei - ste - rin, lasst mich in Frie - den wei - ter - ziehn, lasst

nie - mals fiel das Wan - dern ein, das Wan - dern.
stets auf Wan - der - schaft be - dacht, das Was - ser!
sich bei Tag nicht mü - de drehn, die Rä - der!
mich in Frie - den wei - ter - ziehn und Wan - dern.

Tape   Read the text of the above song onto a tape, without stopping the tape.

SECTION 2: *ä*

[ε]

In singing, the letter *ä* is usually pronounced [ε], whether long or short, for example, *Händel* [ˈhɛndəl].

Exercise 9.3

Pronounce the following words containing *ä*:

1. Händel, Götterdämmerung, Ländler, Bäcker
2. Jäger, Hähne, Mädchen, krähen, wählen
3. dämpfen, ändern, ängstlich, Ärger, fährt
4. Bäche, lästern, Verräter, Blätter, Nächte

Excerpts

Read the following excerpts aloud:

1. Väter, lasst euch's Warnung sein,
   sperrt die Zuckerplätzchen ein!
   sperrt die jungen Mädchen ein!

   Warnung
   Mozart

2. Du Doppelgänger, du bleicher Geselle!
   Was äffst du nach mein Liebesleid
   das mich gequält auf dieser Stelle
   so manche Nacht, in alter Zeit?

   Der Doppelgänger
   Schubert

3. Ängste, quäle
   Dich nicht länger, meine Seele!
   Freu dich! schon sind da und dorten
   Morgenglocken wach geworden.

   In der Frühe
   Wolf

Song

Die Gedanken sind frei

Die Ge - dan - ken sind __ frei! Wer __ kann sie er -
Ich den - ke was ich will, und __ was mich be -
Ich lie - be den __ Wein, mein __ Mäd - chen vor
Drum will ich auf __ im - mer den __ Sor - gen ent -

ra - ten? Sie flie - hen vor - bei wie __ nächt - li - che
glük - ket, doch al - les in der Still' und __ wie es sich
al - len, sie tut mir al - lein am __ be - sten ge -
sa - gen und will mich auch __ nim - mer mit __ Gril - len mehr

Schat - ten. Kein Mensch kann sie wis - sen, kein Jä - ger er -
schik - ket. Mein Wunsch, mein Be - geh - ren kann nie - mand mir
fal - len. Ich sitz' nicht al - lei - ne bei mei - nem Glas
pla - gen. Man kann ja im Her - zen stets la - chen und

schie - ssen, es blei - bet da - bei: die Ge - dan - ken sind frei.
weh - ren, es blei - bet da - bei: die Ge - dan - ken sind frei.
Wei - ne, mein Mäd - chen da - bei: die Ge - dan - ken sind frei.
scher - zen und den - ken da - bei: die Ge - dan - ken sind frei.

SECTION 3: *ie*

[i]

Except under the conditions outlined below, *ie* is pronounced [i]: *die* [di] (the), *fliegen* ['fligən] (fly).

Final -*ie* [i]

In some words of foreign origin, final -*ie* is stressed and pronounced [i], as in *Melodie* [melo'di]. Many of these words are scientific, such as *Geographie, Philosophie*. However, the singer should become familiar with the following examples:

Elegie	Partie ("passage"
Galerie	or "game")
Genie	Phantasie
Melancholie	Poesie
Melodie	Symphonie

Final -*ie* [jə]

In other words of foreign origin, final -*ie* is unaccented and pronounced [jə], as in *Familie* [fɑ'miljə]. The singer should learn to recognize the following words of this type:

Akazie	Historie
Arie	Hortensie
Bestie	Hostie
Dahlie	Kamelie
Familie	Kastanie
Fuchsie	Komödie
Gardenie	Lilie
Glorie	Pinie
Linie	Tragödie
Grazie	

Final *-ien* [iən]

In the plurals of words of the type *Melodie*, final *-ien* is pronounced [iən] and the stress is on the next to last syllable: *Melodien* [melo'diən].

Final *-ien* [jən]

In the plurals of words of the type *Familie* the stress falls on the same syllable as in the singular, and final *-ien* is pronounced [jən]: *Familien* [fɑ'miljən]. Also in geographical names, *-ien* is pronounced [jən], for example, *Belgien* ['bɛlgjən]. The following examples might occur in vocal literature:

Asien
Belgien
Indien
Italien
Spanien

Exercise 9.4

Pronounce the following words:

1. Lied, fliessen, riechen, Ziel, studieren
2. Kastanien, Melodien, verdient, Lilien, fliehen
3. Spanien, Symphonie, probieren, Begierde, Brief
4. Partie, Glorie, Riemen, wieder, Priester
5. liegen, Pinien, liebt, hielt, hier, schrie

Excerpts

Read the following excerpts aloud:

1. Die Rose, die Lilie, die Taube, die Sonne,
   Die liebt' ich einst alle in Liebeswonne.

   Dichterliebe
   Schumann

2. Erzeugt von heisser Phantasie,
   In einer schwärmerischen Stunde zur Welt gebrachte,
   Geht zu Grunde, ihr Kinder der Melancholie!

   Als Luise die Briefe
   Mozart

Tape

Read the following song text onto a tape without stopping the recorder:

Rosen brach ich nachts mir am dunklen Hage;
Süsser hauchten Duft sie als je am Tage,
Doch verstreuten reich die bewegten Äste
    Tau, der mich nässte.

Auch der Küsse Duft mich wie nie berückte,
Die ich nachts vom Strauch deiner Lippen pflückte;
Doch auch dir, bewegt im Gemüt gleich jenen,
    Tauten die Tränen!

Sapphische Ode
Brahms

Chapter 10 | The Sounds of *s* and Its Combinations

SECTION 1: *s*

[z]

Before a vowel, *s* is pronounced [z], as in *singen* ['zIŋən] (sing), *einsam* ['ɑenzɑm] (lonely).

When *s* occurs before *l, n,* or *r* in an inflected form or derivative of a word ending in *-el, -en,* or *-er,* it is pronounced [z], as in *unsre* ['Unzɾə] (< *unser*).

Exceptions

In a few words, *s* is voiceless after a voiceless consonant, even though it precedes a vowel. Learn to recognize the following:

Erbse ['ɛrpsə]	(pea)
Krebse ['krepsə]	(crabs)
Rätsel ['rɛtsel]	(riddle)

[s]

When *s* appears before a consonant, at the end of a word, or at the end of an element, it is pronounced [s], as in *Dresden* ['drɛsdən], *Betrugs* [bə'truks] (deceit), *Lesart* ['les,ʔart] (version), *Grashalm* ['grɑs,hɑlm][1] (blade of grass).

Exercise 10.1   Contrast voiced and unvoiced *s* in the following pairs of related words:

1. kreisen   Kreis
2. Halse   Hals
3. Speise   speist
4. Hause   Haus
5. lösen   löst
6. lesen   lesbar

---

[1] Note that in German *s* and *h* do not form a combination as in English. When they appear together, they always represent parts of two different elements and are thus pronounced as [s] + [h].

Exercise 10.2 Pronounce the following words, observing the rules for pronunciation of *s*:

1. Sage, Wiese, böse, Schicksal, seltsam
2. dies, diesen, Jesus, als, Felsen, kraus
3. gesät, Glas, Abendsonne, löst, Amsel, Friedenshaus
4. Hungersnot, Feinslieb, Königs, Guts, Rose, Linse
5. Ratsherrn, Frühlingsabendrot, heisre, holdselig
6. gesund, ringsum, losgebe, Mannsbild, Asyl
7. auserkorn, Himmelslust, boshaft, Hausarzt, Röslein
8. Todesangst, Gotteserde, gottselig, Insel, Rätsel, emsige

ss

Simple Words

The combination *ss,* also spelled ß or *sz* under certain conditions,[2] is pronounced [s] when it appears in a simple word, e.g. *müssen* ['mYsən] (must), *muß* [mUs] (must), *mußte* ['mUstə] (had to).

Compounds

If an element ending in *s* is followed by an element beginning with *s*, then the first *s* is not voiced. The second *s* is pronounced according to the conditions in the second element, for example, *Aussage* ['aos,zagə], *aussteigen* ['aos,ʃtaegən]. (See also Sections 2 and 3 below.)

Exercise 10.3 Contrast *s* and *ss* (ß) in the following pairs:

1. Fliesen   fließen
2. Weise   weiße
3. Nase   nasse
4. Rose   Rosse

---

[2] The symbol ß is not normally used in scores printed in this country. It will be used in this chapter only, in order to familiarize the student with it.

ß is used in the following positions:

1. at the end of a word or element: muß, Gruß, Gußeisen
2. before a consonant: müßte, grüßte
3. intervocalically after a *long* vowel: grüßen

ß does not appear intervocalically after a short vowel: *müssen;* note that in positions 1 and 2, ß may appear after either a long or a short vowel.

ß may also appear in some scores as *sz.* The pronunciation will remain [s], for example, *auszen* ['aosən], provided of course that *s* and *z* do not belong to two different elements, as in *Auszug* ['aos,tsuk].

Exercise 10.4

Pronounce the following pairs of words, noting the contrast in the vowels preceding *ss* and ß:

1. Busse   Buße
2. schlossen   Schloßen
3. flösse   Flöße
4. Flüsse   Füße

Exercise 10.5

Pronounce the following words, observing the rules for pronunciation of *ss* (ß):

1. Wasser, essen, vermissen, draußen, heißen
2. müssen, muß, mußte, müßte, fließen
3. grüßen, Gruß, grüßte, süß, süße
4. Geheimnisse, Waldessaume, dasselbe, besessen
5. Aussätzigen, fesselte, weissagen, mißachten
6. lossagen, Drossel, Liebessehnsucht, Mißverständnis

Excerpts

1. Allnächtlich im Traume seh' ich dich,
   Und sehe dich freundlich grüßen,
   Und laut aufweinend stürz' ich mich
   Zu deinen süßen Füßen.

   Dichterliebe
   Schumann

2. Ich saß zu deinen Füßen in Waldeseinsamkeit;
   Windesatmen, Sehnen ging durch die Wipfel breit.
   In stummem Ringen senkt' ich das Haupt in deinen Schoß,
   Und meine bebenden Hände um deine Knie ich schloß.
   Die Sonne ging hinunter, der Tag verglühte all,
   Ferne, sang eine Nachtigall, sang eine Nachtigall.

   In Waldeseinsamkeit
   Brahms

Song

Sing the following song, paying close attention to the pronunciation of *s*.

Wir sind jung

Wir sind jung, die Welt ist of - fen, o du schö - ne, wei - te
Liegt dort hin - ter je - nem Wal - de nicht ein fer - nes, frem - des
Auf denn, auf! die Son - ne zei - ge uns den Weg durch Wald und

Welt! Uns - re Sehn - sucht, un - ser Hof - fen zielt hin -
Land? Blüht auf grü - ner Ber - ges - hal - de nicht das
Hain; geht der Tag dar - ob zur Nei - ge, leuch - te

aus in Wald und Feld. Bru - der, lass den Kopf nicht
Blüm - lein un - be - kannt? Lasst uns schrei - ten im Ge -
uns der Ster - ne Schein. Bru - der, schnell den Ruck - sack

hän - gen,   kannst ja   nicht   die Ster - ne   sehn!   Auf - wärts
län - de,   ü - ber   Tä - ler ü - ber   Höh'n!   Wo   sich
ü - ber,   heu - te   soll's   ins Wei - te   gehn.   Re - gen?

blik - ken, vor - wärts drän - gen!   Wir sind   jung   und das   ist   schön!
auch   der Weg   hin - wen - de: Wir sind   jung   und das   ist   schön!
Wind?   wir la - chen   drü - ber: Wir sind   jung   und das   ist   schön!

SECTION 2: *st, sp*

[ʃt], [ʃp]

When *st* and *sp* appear at the beginning of a word or element, they are pronounced
[ʃt] and [ʃp], as in *stellen* ['ʃtɛlən] (place), *versprechen* [fɛɒ'ʃprɛçən] (promise).

 Exercise 10.6   Pronounce the following words:

     1. stellen, Stück, aufstellen, verstehen, Gestalt
     2. spinnen, Sprache, aufspalten, versprechen, Gespenst

[st], [sp]

In all other cases, *st* and *sp* are pronounced [st] and [sp].

Specifically, they are [st] and [sp] in simple words when they do not appear at the beginning of an element, for example, in *beste* ['bɛstə] (best), *ist* [Ist] (is).

They are, of course, [st] and [sp] if the letters belong to different elements, as in *ausprägen* ['aos,prɛgən] (stamp), *austragen* ['aos,tragən] (carry out).

The superlative suffix -*st* is pronounced [st] regardless of what ending follows it: *schnellste* ['ʃnɛlstə], *schnellstes* ['ʃnɛlstəs] (fastest).

Exercise 10.7   Pronounce the following words:

1. Liste, Westen, austeilen, wärmste, wärmsten
2. Wespe, Espe, auspacken, Liebespaar

Exercise 10.8   Contrast [ʃt] and [st] in words of similar appearance:

1. Gestirn   gestern
2. bestehen   besten
3. erstehen   ersten

Exercise 10.9   Pronounce the words below, following the rules for pronunciation of *st* and *sp:*

1. stehen, spät, entstehen, besprechen, zustoßen
2. lispeln, rasten, finster, Meister, schnellste
3. Strand, löste, schlugst, zuerst, Saitenspiel
4. hinsterbend, bestrebt, bester, hineinstehlen, Ostern
5. erspähen, feste, Festung, sturmestot, wegstehlen
6. liebestrunkene, Waldstrom, sternebesäeten, betrügst
7. strömt, speist, Liebeston, fernste, Wanderstab, Trost
8. unheiligster, Wehmutsstrahlen, Dienstag, Diebstahl, Fenster
9. Todestag, durchspielen, seligsten, Edelstein, erstreiten
10. Versuchungsplagen, einstürzen, Waldespracht, Hammerstreich
11. huldreichstes, Liebestraum, Festrede, Garnstricker, Gaststätte
12. Gesangstunde, Gestade, gestern, Geste, gestehen, Gerstenstange
13. garstig, Gottestisch, Götterspeise, Grabstein, Fistelstimme
14. heraustritt, Himmelstrank, Singestuhl, Singstunde, desto
15. Abendstern, Muster, Austausch, austreiben, Beständigkeit
16. Baumstamm, Beispiel, Bernstein, Betstunde, schönster, düster
17. Ruhestätte, Todesstoß, Künstler, Todespein, Siegespreis

Excerpts

1. Und zu dem Strand, dem weiten, wogenblauen,
   Werden wir still und langsam niedersteigen.

   Morgen
   Strauss

2. In deine Decke grab' ich
   Mit einem spitzen Stein
   Den Namen meiner Liebsten
   Und Stund' and Tag hinein.

   Winterreise
   Schubert

3. Wie anders hast du mich empfangen,
   Du Stadt der Unbeständigkeit!
   In deinen blanken Fenstern sangen
   Die Lerch' und Nachtigall im Streit.

   Winterreise
   Schubert

4. Sahst du sie gestern Abend nicht am Tore stehn,
   Mit langem Halse nach der grossen Strasse sehn?
   Wenn von dem Fang der Jäger lustig zieht nach Haus,
   Da steckt kein sittsam Kind den Kopf zum Fenster 'naus.

   Eifersucht und Stolz
   Schubert

5. Zwar ist solche Herzensstube
   Wohl kein schöner Fürstensaal,
   Sondern eine finstre Grube;
   Doch, sobald dein Gnadenstrahl
   In dieselbe nur wird blinken,
   Wird sie voller Sonnen dünken.

   Christmas Oratorio
   Bach

SECTION 3: *sch*

[ʃ]

In simple words, *sch* is pronounced [ʃ]: *Schule* ['ʃulə] (school), *schräg* [ʃrɛk] (crooked), *schlagen* ['ʃlagən] (beat), *rasch* [raʃ] (quickly).

[sç]

When *s* and *ch* appear together as parts of two different elements, they will be pronounced separately. In this situation, *s* appears at the end of an element and is unvoiced. Usually, the following element will be the diminutive suffix *-chen,* and *ch* will be pronounced [ç]: *Röschen* ['røsçən] (little rose).

Exercise 10.10

Pronounce the following words, following the rules for pronunciation of *sch:*

1. Schiff, schmal, schlugst, Kirsche, Kirche
2. löschen, frischem, Häschen, herrschen, Dornröschen
3. Herrschaft, Austausch, ausschwärmen, Glasscherbe
4. Bläschen, Lieschen, Geschichte, Gotteshaus, Esche
5. dreschen, verschmelzen, Grashalm, boshaft, durchschleichen

Exercise 10.11

Read the following transcription aloud:
[ɑχ, Iç fyls, ɛs ʔIst fɛɒ'ʃvUndən,
'evIç hIn deɒ 'libə glYk!
'nImɒ kɔmt ʔiɒ 'vɔnə,ʃtUndən
'mɑenəm 'hɛrtsən meɒ tsu'rYk.
zi, tɑ'mino, 'dizə 'trɛnən 'flisən,
'trɑotɒ, diɒ ʔɑ'lɑen.
fylst du nIçt deɒ 'libə 'zenən,
zo vIrt ru ʔIm 'todə zɑen.]

Excerpts

Read the following excerpts aloud, paying special attention to the sounds of *s* and its combinations:

1. O liebliche Wangen,
   Ihr macht mir Verlangen,
   Dies rote, dies weisse
   Zu schauen mit Fleisse.
   Und dies nur alleine
   Ist's nicht, was ich meine;
   Zu schauen, zu grüssen,
   Zu rühren, zu küssen!
   Ihr macht mir Verlangen,
   O liebliche Wangen!
   O Sonne der Wonne!
   O Wonne der Sonne!
   O Augen, so saugen
   Das Licht meiner Augen.
   O englische Sinnen!

O himmlisch Beginnen!
O Himmel auf Erden!
Magst du mir nicht werden,
O Wonne der Sonne,
O Sonne der Wonne!
O Schönste der Schönen!
Benimm mir dies Sehnen,
Komm eile, komm, komme,
Du Süsse, du Fromme!
Ach Schwester, ich sterbe,
Ich sterb', ich verderbe,
Komm, komme, komm eile,
Komm, komme, komm eile,
Benimm mir dies Sehnen,
O Schönste der Schönen.

O liebliche Wangen
Brahms

2. O du, für den ich alles trug,
Könnt' ich zur Stelle dringen,
Wo Bosheit dich in Fesseln schlug,
Und süssen Trost dir bringen!

Fidelio
Beethoven

Tape

Read the following song text onto a tape without stopping the recorder:

Meine Liebe ist grün wie der Fliederbusch,
Und mein Lieb ist schön wie die Sonne;
Die glänzt wohl herab auf den Fliederbusch
Und füllt ihn mit Duft und mit Wonne.

Meine Seele hat Schwingen der Nachtigall
Und wiegt sich in blühendem Flieder,
Und jauchzet und singet vom Duft berauscht
Viel liebestrunkene Lieder.

Meine Liebe ist Grün
Brahms

Song

Sing the following song, paying special attention to the pronunciation of *s* and its combinations.

Wem Gott will rechte Gunst

Wem Gott will rech - te Gunst er - wei - sen, den
Die Bäch - lein von den Ber - gen sprin - gen, die
Den lie - ben Gott lass ich nur wal - ten, der

schickt - er in die wei - te Welt, dem_ will er sei - ne Wun - der
Ler - chen schwir - ren hoch vor Lust. Wie_ sollt ich nicht mit ih - nen
Bäch - lein, Ler - chen, Wald und Feld und_ Erd' und Him - mel will er -

wei - sen in Berg und Tal und Strom und Feld.
sin - gen aus vol - ler Kehl und fri - scher Brust.
hal - ten, hat auch mein Sach aufs best be - stellt.

Chapter 11 | Diphthongs

SECTION 1: *au*

[ɑo]

The German diphthong [ɑo], as in *Haus* [hɑos] is often equated with the English diphthong [aU], as in *house* [haUs]. As the symbols indicate, the substitution is not quite justified. The English diphthong begins with the front vowel [a], whereas the German sound begins with the back vowel [ɑ]. The English diphthong ends with the open vowel [U]; the German diphthong ends with the more closed vowel [o].

Exercise 11.1   Pronounce the following words:

1. Maus, Laus, Faust, lauschen, hinauslaufen
2. rauschen, Pause, Schmaus, austauschen, auflegen

Excerpt

Es rauschen die Wipfel und schauern,
Als machten zu dieser Stund'
Um die halbversunkenen Mauern
Die alten Götter die Rund'.

Schöne Fremde
Schumann

SECTION 2: *ei*

[ɑe]

The sound of German *ei*,[1] as in *mein* [mɑen] (my), is similar to the English diphthong [aI] in *mine* [maIn], but more closed, more clipped—hence the closed vowel [e] rather than the open vowel [I] in its transcription.

The singer should be exceptionally careful not to confuse *ei* with *ie*. The

---

[1] Alternate, and usually older, spellings of this diphthong include *ai, ey,* and *ay: Mai, Meyer, Bayern.*

two are never pronounced the same. Even if they occur in different forms of the same verb, *ei* is pronounced [ɑe] and *ie* is pronounced [i]: *schreibt* [ʃrɑept] (writes), *schriebt* [ʃript] (wrote).

Exercise 11.2

Pronounce the following words:

1. Eiche, beichten, Geige, aussteigen, Kaiser
2. Heide, Waise, Weise, Wiese, Hain, Bayreuth
3. gleich, Maid, Freiheit, Saite, Seite
4. schreien, schrieen, gedeihen, gediehen, feiern

Excerpts

1. Und ich geh mit Einer, die mich lieb hat,
   Ruhigen Gemütes in die Kühle
   Dieses weissen Hauses, in den Frieden,
   Der voll Schönheit wartet, dass wir kommen.

   Freundliche Vision
   Strauss

2. Heiss mich nicht reden, heiss mich schweigen,
   Denn mein Geheimnis ist mir Pflicht;
   Ich möchte dir mein ganzes Innre zeigen,
   Allein das Schicksal will es nicht.

   Mignon 2
   Wolf

Tape

Make a tape recording of the following song:

Die Rose, die Lilie, die Taube, die Sonne,
Die lieb' ich einst alle in Liebeswonne.
Ich lieb' sie nicht mehr, ich liebe alleine
Die Kleine, die Feine, die Reine, die Eine;
Sie selber, aller Liebe Bronne,
Ist Rose und Lilie und Taube und Sonne.

Dichterliebe
Schumann

Song

Sing the following song, paying close attention to the pronunciation of *ei*.

Ihr kleinen Vögelein

Ihr klei - nen_ Vö - ge - lein, ihr Wald - er - göt - zer - lein, ihr sü - ssen
Spitzt eu - re_ Schnä - be - lein, zwingt eu - re Stim - me - lein und fangt als_
Er ziert euch Feld und Wald so schön und man - nig - falt. Er kleidt euch
Drum stim - met_ mit mir ein, ihr sü - ssen Schrei - er - lein ihr klei - nen

Sän - ger - lein, stimmt al - le mit mir_ ein! Ich
gross und_ klein, aufs lieb - lich - ste zu_ schrein. Ich
jung und_ alt, mit Fe - dern wohl ge - stalt. Er
Pfei - fer - lein, ihr Wun - der - sän - ger - lein: Gott

will den Her - ren prei - sen mit mei - nen Lie - bes - wei - sen. Ich will von
will durch eu - er Sin - gen mich zu dem Schöp - fer schwin - gen. Ich will durch
schafft euch küh - le Sit - ze für Un - fall und für Hit - ze. Er gibt euch
Lob ist mein Er - schal - len, Gott Lob sei eu'r Er - hal - len. Gott Lob ist

Her - zens - grund ihm auf - tun mei - nen Mund!
eu - ern Ton hin - an zu Got - tes Sohn.
Speis und Trank und Mut zum Lust - ge - sang.
mein Ge - sang, Gott Lob sei eu - er Klang.

SECTION 3: *eu, äu*

Just as the diphthongs *ei* and *au* are pronounced differently from their English equivalents, the German diphthong [ɔø], as in *Fäuste* ['fɔøstə] (fists) is more closed and more rounded than the English diphthong [ɔI] in *foist* [fɔIst]. Both *eu* and *äu* are pronounced [ɔø]: *Leute* ['lɔøtə] (people), *läute* ['lɔøtə] (ring).

Occasionally, *e* and *u* appear together as parts of two different elements, as in *beurteilen (judge);* in such a case, they are of course pronounced separately: [bə'Urtɑelən].

The singer is cautioned particularly about related words containing *au* and *äu,* such as *Haus* [hɑos] (house), *Häuser* ['hɔøzɒ] (houses).

Exercise 11.3 Contrast *au* and *äu* in the following pairs of related words:

1. lauft   läuft
2. Strauss   Sträusse
3. rauben   Räuber
4. Maus   Mäuse

Exercise 11.4 Pronounce the following words:

1. Täufer, Teufel, feucht, leuchten, Säule
2. Bräutigam, Braut, Frau, Fräulein, zeugen
3. liebäugeln, Efeu, beugen, beunruhigen
4. Streuselkuchen, treuster, Feuer, Löwenbräu

Exercise 11.5 Read the following transcription aloud:

ʃo 'kylɒ valt, vo 'rɑoʃəst du,
In dem mɑen 'lipçən get?
o 'vidɒˌhɑl, vo 'lɑoʃəst du,
deɒ gɛrn mɑen lit fɛɒ'ʃtet?
Im hɛrtsən tif dɑ rɑoʃt deɒ valt,
In dem mɑen lipçən get,
In 'ʃmɛrtsən ʃlif deɒ 'vidɒˌhɑl,
di 'lidɒ zInt fɛɒ'vet.]

Excerpts

1. Streuet ihm, Schwestern,
   Streuet ihm Blumen,
   Bringt ihm knospende Rosen dar.
   Aber euch, Schwestern,
   Grüss' ich mit Wehmut,
   Freudig scheidend aus eurer Schar.

   Frauenliebe und Leben
   Schumann

2. Fleuch, Nachtigall, in grüne Finsternisse,
   Ins Haingesträuch,
   Und spend' im Nest der treuen Gattin Küsse;
   Entfleuch, entfleuch!

   An die Nachtigall
   Brahms

3. Unter den Lindenbäumen, die Nachtigall
   Uns zu Häupten soll von unsren Küssen träumen.

   Ständchen
   Strauss

4. Die schönen weissen Wolken ziehn dahin
   Durchs tiefe Blau, wie schöne stille Träume,
   Mir ist, als ob ich längst gestorben bin
   Und ziehe selig mit durch ewge Räume.

   Feldeinsamkeit
   Brahms

Song

Sing the following song, paying special attention to the words containing *eu* and *äu*.

Das Lieben bringt gross Freud

Das   Lie - ben bringt gross' Freud', es __ wis - sen's al - le __
Ein   Brief - lein schrieb sie __ mir, ich __ sollt' treu blei - ben
Mein   ei - gen soll sie __ sein, kei - nem an - dern mehr als __

Leut'.   Weiss __ mir ein schö - nes Schät - ze - lein mit __
ihr.   Drauf __ schickt' ich ihr ein Sträu - sse - lein, schön __
mein.   So __ le - ben wir in Freud __ und __ Leid, bis __

zwei schwarz - brau - nen __ Äu - ge - lein, die __ mir, die __
Ros - ma - rin, __ und __ Nä - ge - lein, sie __ soll, sie __
Gott, der Herr, aus - ein - an - der - scheid't. Dann a - de, dann a -

mir, die_____ mir mein Herz er - freut.
soll, sie_____ soll mein ei - gen_____ sein.
de! Dann a - de, mein Schatz, a - de!

SECTION 4: *Other Vowel Combinations*

In vowel combinations other than those specifically discussed, each member will be pronounced separately: *zuerst* [tsu'ʔɛrst] (first), *Poet* [po'et], etc.

Exercise 11.6   Pronounce the following:

Kreatur   säen
Diamant   böig
Duell   Poesie
ideal

Chapter 12 | The Sounds of l, r

SECTION 1: *l*

[l]

In English the sound [l] is articulated with the tongue cupped downward in the middle and the tip resting on the alveolar ridge, as in *fell* [fɛl]. In German, the sound [l] (no difference in transcription) is articulated with the tongue nearly flat and the tip resting against the upper teeth, as in *Fell* [fɛl] (skin).

Exercise 12.1 Contrast the pronunciation of *l* in the following pairs:

English	German
fell	Fell
Helen	hellen
fleck	Fleck
lope	Lob

ll

Normally, *ll* is pronounced the same as *l*, as in *fällen* ['fɛlən] (fell), although it is often extended somewhat in singing diction. However, when it represents parts of two elements, it is markedly lengthened and divided between notes, as in *fühllos* ['fyllos] (insensitive).

Exercise 12.2 Pronounce the following words:

1. Ball, Lampe, schlau, Schulter, fällen
2. blassen, ablassen, allmächtig, alliebend, Balsam
3. Lieder, Walter, geblichen, vergeblichen, selten
4. wohllautender, Milch, Dolch, solch, gelb, Geld, Klang
5. glich, behaglich, Klavier, tadellos, heillos, bewilligen

Songs Sing the following songs, concentrating on the special articulation of German *l*.

Mein Herz ist voll Lieder

Mein Herz ist voll Lie - der, die See - le voll
Und kä - me mein Schatz mit mir in den

Sang; was ich auch spiel - te ist Froh - sinn, ist Sang; durch
Wald, die Vög - lein al - le, die schwie - gen gar bald, und

Fel - der und Au - en nur ei - ne Me - lo - dei: Mein
lausch - ten auf sei - ne so fro - hen Me - lo - dei'n: Mein

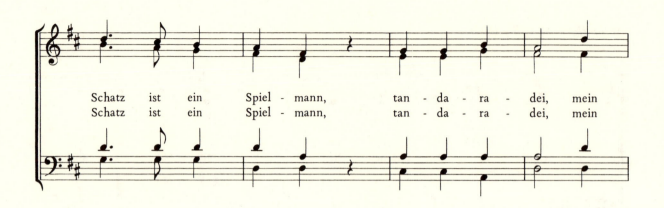

Schatz ist ein Spiel - mann, tan - da - ra - dei, mein
Schatz ist ein Spiel - mann, tan - da - ra - dei, mein

Schatz ist ein Spiel - mann, tan - da - ra - dei.
Schatz ist ein Spiel - mann, tan - da - ra - dei.

Auf der Lüneburger Heide

Auf der Lü - ne - bur - ger Hei - de, in dem
Brü - der lasst die Glä - ser klin - gen, denn der
Und die Hun - de und die bel - len, und die

wun - der - schö - nen___ Land,   ging ich auf und ging___ ich___
Mus - ka - tel - ler___ Wein   wird vom lan - gen Ste - hen___
Büch - se und die___ knallt,   ro - te Hir - sche woll'n wir___

un - ter, al - ler - lei am Weg ich___ fand.   Va - le -
sau - er, aus - ge - trun - ken muss er___ sein.
ja - gen in dem grü - nen grü - nen___ Wald.

ri, va - le - ra, va - le - ri, va - le - ra, und juch -

hei - ras - sa,__ juch - hei - ras - sa, be - ster Schatz, be - ster Schatz, be - ster

Schatz, be - ster Schatz, denn du weisst es, weisst es ja.

SECTION 2: *r (Conclusion)*

Postvocalic *r*

In Chapter 5, the singer was advised to adopt the vowellike sound [ɒ] for the suffix *-er* and for *r* in final position in certain monosyllables and prefixes but to use [ɾ] for *r* in all other positions. It has no doubt become apparent that *no* singer strictly adheres to this differentiation. However, it has probably become equally apparent that no singer uses *only* the one-tap trill. The English-speaking singer, in part influenced by Italian diction, in part for simplicity's sake, tends to use the trill for all *r*'s. This results in an unduly severe sound, especially in the art song. Only by making the somewhat artificial differentiation between [ɾ] and [ɒ] could we encourage the voice student to develop the use of [ɒ].

Now let us review and expand the guidelines for the use of [ɾ] and [ɒ]. Although [ɒ] *may* be used for any final or preconsonantal *r,* it occurs most frequently: (1) in short words, such as pronouns, articles, and possessives, for instance, *mir* [miɒ], *wir* [viɒ], *der* [deɒ], *ihr* [iɒ]; (2) in prefixes ending in *r,* especially before consonants, as in *vergehen* [fɛɒ'geən], *ergreift* [ɛɒ'graeft]; and (3) for unstressed *-er* when it is final or final before a consonant, for instance, *aber* ['abɒ], *besser* ['bɛsɒ], *mildert* ['mIldɒt], *hundert* ['hUndɒt]. *r* is normally trilled: (1) when it appears after a stressed vowel and before a consonant, as in *warten* ['vartən], *fertig* ['fɛrtIç]; (2) when it appears finally in nouns, adjectives, verbs, etc.: *Meer* [mer], *wahr* [var], *fahr'* [far].

The choice of articulation for *r* can be of considerable expressive importance in the interpretation of a song. Many singers use the one-tap trill almost exclusively, especially for baroque music and Wagner. Others prefer to use the trill more sparingly, thereby achieving a softer quality. It is recommended that beginning singers adopt the latter approach. This allows for more effective use of the one-tap trill for emphasis and force.

rr

[ɾ]

In simple words *rr* is usually pronounced [ɾ], rarely [ɒ]: *sperren* ['ʃpɛɾən], *dürr* [dYɾ], *irrt* [Iɾt].

[ɒɾ]

When *rr* represents parts of two elements it is usually pronounced [ɒɾ]: *Vorrede* ['foɒˌɾedə], *erraten* [ɛɒ'ɾɑtən].

    Some singers use an extended trill for *rr* in simple words and compounds as well as for *r* in combinations such as *fr* and *tr*. This articulation should be avoided by the beginner.

Exercise 12.3	Pronounce the following words:

        1. Torheit, ereilt, beerben, dankerfüllten

        2. vereint, wiederholt, Verräter, ehrerbietig, arglos

        3. Meisterehre, Meisterregeln, erreicht, surren

        4. feuerrot, herrlich, herreiten, Irrtum, Winterreise

        5. daran, fortan, hervorrufen, herüberreiten

Exercise 12.4	Transcribe the above words into the IPA.
Songs	Practice the different articulations of *r* by singing the following songs.

Es, es, es und es

Es, es, es und es, es ist ein har - ter Schluss,
Er, er, er und er, Herr Meis - ter leb' er wohl!
Sie, sie, sie und sie, Frau Meis - trin leb' sie wohl!
Ihr, ihr, ihr und ihr, ihr Jung - fern le - bet wohl!

Wohlan, die Zeit ist kommen

Wohl - an, die Zeit ist kom - men, mein Pferd, das muss ge -
In mei - nes Va - ters Gar - ten, da stehn viel schö - ne
Du glaubst du wärst die Schön - ste wohl auf der gan - zen
Der Kai - ser streit fürs Länd - le, der Her - zog für sein
So - lang ich leb auf Er - den, sollst du mein Trim - ple -

sat - telt sein; ich hab mir's vor - ge - nom - men, ge -
Blum, ja Blum. Drei Jahr muss ich noch war - ten, drei
Welt, ja Welt, und auch die An - ge - nehm - ste, ist
Geld, ja Geld, und ich streit für mein Schätz - le, so -
Tram - ple sein, und wenn ich einst ge - stor - ben bin, so

rit - ten muss es sein!
Jahr sind bald her - um.
a - ber weit ge - fehlt! Geh du nur hin, ich
lang es mir ge - fällt.
tram - pelst hin - ter - drein.

hab mein Teil, ich lieb dich nur aus Nar - re - tei; oh - ne

dich kann ich wohl le - ben, oh - ne dich kann ich schon sein.

Chapter 13 | The Sounds of h, j

SECTION 1: *h*

Silent

In general, *h* is not pronounced after a vowel, unless it begins an element.[1] Specifically, postvocalic *h* is silent: (1) at the end of a word or element: *Floh* [flo] (flea), *Gehrock* ['ge͵rɔk] (coat); (2) before a consonant: *steht* [ʃtet] (stands); (3) before a vowel: *gehen* ['geən] (go). Occasionally singers, even the best, pronounce the *h* in a slow passage in a word like *gehen:* ['gehən]. This is not desirable and sounds affected. However, this situation is not to be confused with that in which *h* begins a new element.

[h]

The voiceless glottal fricative [h] is used for *h* at the beginning of a word or element: *Hand* [hɑnt] (hand), *gehört* [gə'høʀt] (heard). It is sometimes difficult for the novice to determine whether *h* begins an element: for example, *froher* (merry) is made up of *froh + er* and is pronounced ['froɒ], whereas *woher* (whence) is made up of *wo + her* and is pronounced [vo'heɒ]. The following words, which can prove troublesome, should be memorized:

behende [bə'hɛndə]	(quick)
woher [vo'heɒ]	(whence)
daher [dɑ'heɒ]	(from there)

Exercise 13.1

Pronounce the following words, observing the rules for pronunciation of *h:*

1. ruhen, ehe, eher, fliehen, Halle, Kindheit
2. hoher, woher, jähes, bisher, einher, wohin
3. geheim, Gehege, gehende, behende, Freiheit
4. Friedhof, gehorchen, Höhe, höhere, Hoheit, allhier
5. wiederholt, dahin, behutsam, abhanden
6. Gotteshaus, Drehorgel, Strohhalm, unbarmherzig

[1] See Chapter 14 for a discussion of *th*.

Excerpts

> 1. Schon krähen die Hähne, und nah ist der Ort.
>   Wohl seh ich, Herrin, der Kraft dir schwinden.
>
> *Nun wandre, Maria*
> Wolf

> 2. Fort in die Freiheit!
>   Dahin gehör' ich,
>   Da, wo ich Meister im Haus!
>
> *Die Meistersinger*
> Wagner

SECTION 2: *j*

[j]

In most words, *j* is pronounced as the voiced palatal fricative (or glide) [j]: *Jammer* ['jɑmɒ] (woe), *bejahen* [bə'jɑən] (affirm), *Major* [mɑ'joɾ] (major), *Kajak* ['kɑjɑk] (kayak).

[ʒ]

In a few words of French origin, initial *j* is pronounced as the voiced prepalatal fricative [ʒ]. Learn to recognize the following:

> Jalousie [ʒalu'zi]
> Jakett [ʒɑ'kɛt]
> Jargon [ʒɑɾ'gõ]
> Journal [ʒuɾ'nɑl]

Exercise 13.2

Pronounce the following words:

1. ja, jetzt, jodeln, Majestät, Januar, Jugend
2. Jünger, Journalist, gejagt, Jäger, Jasmin, gejubelt

Chapter 14 | The Sounds of z, p, t, k, x, qu

SECTION 1: *z*

[ts]

The letter *z* is pronounced [ts] in all positions: *Zeit* [tsɑet] (time), *bezahlen* [bə'tsɑlən] (pay), *tanzen* ['tɑntsən] (dance), *Kreuz* [krɔøts] (cross).

zz

[ts]

In words of Italian origin, *zz* is pronounced [ts]: *Skizze* ['skItsə] (sketch), *Intermezzo* [Intɒ'mɛtso].

tz

[ts]

In simple words, *tz* is pronounced the same as *z: setzen* ['zɛtsən] (set), *Schatz* [ʃɑts] (treasure).

[tts]

When *t* belongs to one element and *z* to the next, the [t] is prolonged, as in *entzücken* [ɛnt'tsYkən] (charm).

Exercise 14.1 Pronounce the following words:

1. Platz, Nutzen, trotz, jetzt, Spezerei, gezeigt
2. Zimmer, Frauenzimmer, Zoo, Zürich, zogst
3. verzichten, Wurzel, stürzt, jauchzen, spazieren
4. Walzer, Lenz, Holz, kreuzigten, Geächze
5. Erzengel, erziehen, erzürnt, herzlos, herziehen
6. zitternd, Zephyr, zusammen, herzerschütternd

Excerpts

> 1. Und nichts zu forschen, nichts zu spähn,
>   Und nur zu träumen leicht und lind,
>   Der Zeiten Wandel nicht zu sehn,
>   Zum zweiten Mal ein Kind!
>
> *O wüsst' ich doch den Weg zurück*
> Brahms

> 2. Da tanzt den Hochzeitreigen
>   Die Herzallerliebste mein.
>
> *Dichterliebe*
> Schumann

Tape

Make a tape recording of the following song:

> Es grünet ein Nussbaum vor dem Haus,
> Duftig,
> Luftig
> Breitet er blättrig die Äste aus.
>
> Viel liebliche Blüten stehen dran;
> Linde
> Winde
> Kommen, sie herzlich zu umfahn.
>
> Es flüstern je zwei zu zwei gepaart,
> Neigend,
> Beugend
> Zierlich zum Kusse die Häuptchen zart.
>
> Sie flüstern von einem Mägdlein, das
> Dächte
> Nächte
> Tagelang, wüsste, ach! selber nicht was.
>
> Sie flüstern,—wer mag verstehn so gar
> Leise
> Weise?
> Flüstern von Bräut'gam und nächstem Jahr.
>
> Das Mägdlein horchet, es rauscht im Baum;
> Sehnend,
> Wähnend,
> Sinkt es lächelnd in Schlaf und Traum.
>
> *Der Nussbaum*
> Schumann

Song   Sing the following song, concentrating on the pronunciation of *z*.

Morgen muss ich fort

Mor - gen muss ich fort von hier und muss Ab - schied
Wenn zwei gu - te Freun - de sind, die ein - an - der
Küs - set dir ein Lüf - te - lein Wan - gen o - der

neh - men; o du al - ler - schön - ste Zier, Schei - den, das____ bringt
ken - nen, Sonn' und Mond be - we - gen sich, e - he sie____ sich
Hän - de, den - ke, dass es Seuf - zer sind, die ich zu____ dir

Grä - men. Da ich dich so treu ge - liebt
tren - nen. Noch viel grö - sser ist der Schmerz,
sen - de; tau - send schick ich täg - lich aus,

ü - ber al - le Ma — ssen, soll ich dich ver -
wenn ein treu ver - lieb - tes Herz in die Frem - de
die da we - hen um dein Haus, weil ich dein ge -

las - sen,___ sol ich___ dich ver las - sen.
zie - het,___ in die___ Frem - de zie - het.
den - ke,___ weil ich___ dein ge - den - ke.

SECTION 2: *p*

[p]

As in English, *p* usually represents the voiceless bilabial stop [p]: *Pein* [pɑen] (pain), *geprahlt* [gə'prɑlt] (boasted).

pp

[p]

Since *pp* does not normally occur at the junction of two elements in a compound, we can say that it is usually pronounced the same as *p*: *Lippe* ['lIpə] (lip), *Suppe* ['zUpə] (soup), *schnappt* [ʃnɑpt] (snaps). Some feel that the sound should be extended slightly when it appears between vowels.

pf

[pf]

The combination *pf* always represents the affricate [pf]. When it occurs at the beginning of a word or element, as in *Pfad* [pfɑt], (path), *gepfiffen* [gə'pfIfən] (whistled), it is launched as a unit on the same note. If it occurs intervocalically in a simple word, such as *Apfel* ['ɑpfəl] (apple), the [p] is usually begun on one beat and released as [f] on the next. The singer must be careful to sound the [p] in this combination.

Exercise 14.2   Pronounce:

Pfeife	tapfer
Pferd	Gipfel
Pflanze	klopfen

ps

[ps]

The combination *ps* is always pronounced [ps], even at the beginning of a word: *Psalm* [psɑlm].

ph

[f]

The combination *ph* is normally pronounced [f], as in *Phrase* ['frɑzə].

Exercise 14.3   Pronounce:

1. Palme, Treppe, Doppelgänger, Pinie, Puppe
2. Pfeil, Pflaume, Schnaps, Phantasie, Prächtig
3. Posten, Pfosten, Pfriem, verpflichten, schlüpfen
4. gepflückt, Psyche, Prophet, Phönix, Pappeln, Sphären

Excerpts.

1. Die Trommel gerühret, das Pfeifchen gespielt!
   Mein Liebster gewaffnet dem Haufen befiehlt,
   Die Lanze hoch führet, die Leute regieret.
   Wie klopft mir das Herz! Wie wallt mir das Blut!

   Die Trommel gerühret
   Beethoven

2. Mit Tritten wie Tritte der Elfen so sacht,
Um über die Blumen zu hüpfen,
Flieg' leicht hinaus in die Mondscheinnacht
Zu mir in den Garten zu schlüpfen.

Ständchen
Strauss

3. Flieg her zum Krippelein,
Flieg her, gefiedert Schwesterlein,
Blas an den feinen Psalterlein,
Sing, Nachtigall, gar fein!

Wach, Nachtigall, wach auf!
Folk Song

Song

Sing the following song, concentrating on the pronunciation of *p* and its combinations.

Der Apfel ist nicht gleich am Baum

Blü - ten - schaum. Da war erst lau - ter
Ta - ges Müh'n, sie sang ihr A - bend -
Fin - ger pfeif: da sind die er - sten
hell ___ und klar. So run - det sich das

Früh - lings - traum und lau - ter Lieb ___ und Gü - te.
lied ___ gar kühn. Und auch bei Re - gen - wet - ter.
Äp - fel reif, und ha - ben ro - te Bak - ken.
Ap - fel - jahr. Und mehr ist nicht ___ zu sa - gen.

SECTION 3: *t*

[t]

As in English, *t* usually represents the voiceless alveolar stop [t]: *Tal* [tɑl] (valley), *beten* ['betən] (pray).

tt

[t]

In simple words, such as *Betten* ['bɛtən] (beds), *Fittich* ['fItIç] (wing), *tt* is usually pronounced [t].

[tt]

When *tt* represents parts of two elements, as in *Bettag* ['bet,tɑk] (day of prayer), it is pronounced [tt].

th

[t]

When *th* does not represent parts of different elements, it is pronounced [t]. In modern German, *th* appears in only a few words which are not compounds, for example, *Theater* [te'ɑtɒ], *Apotheke* [ɑpo'tekə].

Musical scores often keep the archaic spelling *th* for *t*, as in *Rath* [rɑt] (modern: *Rat*) (counsel), *Theil* [tael] (modern: *Teil*) (part).

[th]

In a number of words, *th* represents parts of two elements in a compound. Since in this case *h* begins an element, it is pronounced, as in *Rathaus* ['rɑt‚hɑos] (town hall).

tsch

[tʃ]

The combination *tsch* represents the affricate [tʃ], as in *Deutsch* [dɔøtʃ].

ti

[tsi]

In a number of words of Latin origin, *ti* is pronounced [tsi]. The only members of this group which might be of interest to the singer are those containing the syllable *-tion*, e.g. *Nation* [nɑ'tsion], *Aktion* [ɑk'tsion].

Exercise 14.4

Pronounce the following words, observing the rules for the pronunciation of *t* and its combinations:

1. Tat, Atem, Schatten, Retter, Hüte, Hütte
2. Auktion, Thema, rotglühend, Therese, dritte
3. enttäuschen, muthig, Thränen, dorthin, Guttat
4. entrauschen, welthellsichtig, Thor, Festtag, flattern
5. Blüthendampfe, Posthorn, Beethoven, plätschern
6. Wehmutsstrahlen, Götter, Hauptton, weither, Walther
7. bereithalten, Bettag, Bretter, bitter, rutschen
8. Funktion, Gasthaus, Peitsche, getheilt, enthält
9. Gasthof, Nation, Wehmuthsthränen, Liebeston, Zither
10. gutherzig, mitreisen, Apostel, Ästhetik
11. Äther, liebestrunken, trösten, Elisabeth, Urtheil

Excerpts

1. So war es mein Kuss,
   Der welthellsichtig dich machte?
   Mein volles Liebesumfangen
   lässt dich dann Gottheit erlangen.

   Parsifal
Wagner

2. Noch war kein Tag, wo du und ich
   Nicht theilten unsre Sorgen.
   Auch waren sie für dich und mich
   getheilt leicht zu ertragen;
   Du tröstetest im Kummer mich,
   Ich weint' in deine Klagen . . .

   Ich liebe dich
Beethoven

3. All' solch' dein' Güt' wir preisen,
   Vater ins Himmelsthron,
   Die du uns thust beweisen,
   durch Christum, deinen Sohn,
   und bitten ferner dich:
   gieb uns ein friedlich's Jahre,
   für allem Leid bewahre
   und nähr' uns mildiglich.

   Zeuch ein zu deinen Toren
Bach

SECTION 4: *k*

[k]

The letter *k* is always pronounced [k]: *kaum* [kɑom] (hardly), *krumm* [krUm] (crooked), *beklagen* [bə'klɑgən] (complain).

kn

[kn]

Unlike in English, the *k* is always pronounced in *kn: Knabe* ['knɑbə] (lad), *geknüpft* [gə'knYpft] (knotted).

ck

[k]

The combination *ck* is pronounced [k]: *nicken* ['nIkən] (nod), *steckt* [ʃtɛkt] (sticks).

   When a word must be divided at *ck* in a musical score, it is spelled *k-k: lok-ki-gen = lockigen.*

kk

[k]

kk appears in only a few words which are not compounds. In these words, which are usually of foreign origin, *kk* is pronounced [k], for example, *Akkord* [ɑˈkɔrt].

[kk]

Usually, *kk* represents parts of two elements, often in the form *ck-k*, and thus is pronounced [kk], as in *Rückkehr* [ˈrʏkˌker] (return).

Exercise 14.5

Pronounce:

1. Kahn, Kinn, kühl, Kur, verkaufen
2. Bäcker, versteckte, frohlocken, Hecken, Backofen
3. eklig, Knopf, akkurat, Schmuckkasten
4. Pauke, Onkel, Birke, Schurke, Schalk
5. Waldecke, entrückte, Droschke, glücklich, zurückkehren
6. Edikt, Kerker, kräftig, Sklave, Knackwurst
7. knüpfen, geknallt, Knie, Knospe, verkniffen
8. gekleidet, Kümmel, Klee, geklebt, klopft, Häkchen

Excerpts

1. Knusper, knusper, Knäuschen,
   Wer knuspert mir am Häuschen.

   Hänsel und Gretel
   Humperdinck

2. Petrus, der nicht denkt zurück,
   Seinen Gott verneinet,
   Der doch auf ein'n ernsten Blick
   Bitterlichen weinet:
   Jesu, blicke mich auch an,
   Wenn ich nicht will büssen;
   Wenn ich Böses hab' gethan,
   Rühre mein Gewissen.

   Jesu Leiden, Pein und Tod
   Bach

Song

Sing the following song, paying attention to the words containing *k* and its combinations.

Es wohnt ein Kaiser an dem Rhein

1. Es wohnt ein Kai - ser an dem Rhein, der hat drei schö - ne Töch - ter -
2. Die er - ste wollt die reich - ste sein, die zwei - te zog ins Klos - ter
3. Die drit - te zog ins frem - de Land, da war sie fremd und un - be -
4. Bei ei - ner Wir - tin klopft sie an, da ward die Tür ihr auf - ge -
5. Wer steht da drau - ssen vor der Tür? Eine ar - me Dienst - magd steht da -
6. So ei - ne Dienst - magd brauch ich nicht, die a - bends vor den Tü - ren
7. Mein Vater ist Kai - ser an dem Rhein, und ich bin Kai - sers Töch - ter -
8. Das konntst du mir schon e - her sagen, ge - stick - te Klei - der konntst du
9. Und als sie nun ge - stor - ben war, drei Lil - ien wuch - sen auf ih - rem

1. lein, Töch - ter - lein, der hat drei schö - ne Töch - ter - lein.
2. ein, Klos - ter ein, die zwei - te zog ins Klos - ter ein.
3. kannt, un - be - kannt, da war sie fremd und un - be - kannt.
4. tan, auf - ge - tan, da ward die Tür ihr auf - ge - tan.
5. für, steht da - für, eine ar - me Dienst - magd steht da - für.
6. liegt, Tü - ren liegt, die a - bends vor den Tü - ren liegt.
7. lein, Töch - ter - lein, und ich bin Kai - sers Töch - ter - lein.
8. tragen, konntst du tragen, ge - stick - te Klei - der konntst du tragen.
9. Grab, ih - rem Grab, drei Lil - ien wuch - sen auf ih - rem Grab.

SECTION 5: *x*

[ks]

As in English, *x* is normally pronounced [ks], as in *Hexe* ['hɛksə] (witch), *Nixe* ['nIksə] (nymph).

qu

[kv]

The combination *qu* is pronounced [kv]: *Quarz* [kvɑrts].

Exercise 14.6

Pronounce:

Qual
Qualität
qualmen
einquartieren
entquellen

Exercise 14.7

Read the following transcription aloud:

[al'nɛçtlIç ˀIm 'trɑomə ze ˀIç dIç
Unt 'zeə dIç 'frɔøntlIç 'grysən
Unt lɑot 'ˀɑof͵vɑenənt ʃtYrts ˀIç mIç
tsu 'dɑenən 'zysən 'fysən
du ziəst mIç ˀɑn 've͵mytIklIç
Unt 'ʃYtəlst dɑs 'blɔndə 'kœpfçən
ɑos 'dɑenən 'ˀɑogən 'ʃlɑeçən zIç
di 'pɛrlən͵trɛnən͵trœpfçən
du zɑkst mɪɒ 'hɑemlIç ˀɑen 'lɑezəs vɔrt,
Unt gipst mɪɒ den ʃtrɑos fɔn tsy'prɛsən
Iç 'vɑxə ˀɑof Unt dɛɒ ʃtrɑos ˀIst fɔrt,
Unts vɔrt hɑp ˀIç fɛɒ'gɛsən

Excerpt

Das heisse Sündenblut entquillt,
ewig erneut aus des Sehnens Quelle.

Parsifal
Wagner

Song

Hänsel und Gretel

Hän - sel und Gre - tel ver - lie - fen sich im Wald.
Hu, hu, da schaut ei - ne al - te He - xe raus!
Doch als die He - xe zum O - fen schaut hin - ein,

Es war so fin - ster und auch so grim - mig kalt. Sie
Lock - te die Kin - der ins Pfef - fer - ku - chen - haus. Sie
ward sie ge - sto - ssen vom Hans und Gre - te - lein. Die

ka - men an ein Häus - chen von Pfef - fer - ku - chen fein:
stell - te sich gar freund - lich o Hän - sel, wel - che Not!
He - xe muss - te bra - ten, die Kin - der gehn nach Haus.

Wer mag der Herr wohl von die - sem Häus - chen sein?
Ihn wollt die bra - ten im O - fen braun wie Brot.
Nun ist das Mär - chen von Hans und Gre - tel aus.

Chapter 15 | The Sounds of c[1]

SECTION 1: *c*

The letter *c* rarely occurs before a vowel in modern German. It does, however, occur in archaic spellings, which are fairly commonly used in song texts.

[ts]

Before a front vowel, *c* is pronounced [ts]: *Citrone* [tsiˈtronə] (lemon), *Cäsar* [ˈtsɛzɑɾ], *cis* [tsis] (C-sharp), *ces* [tsɛs] (C-flat).[2]

[k]

Before a back vowel, *c* is pronounced [k]: *Café* [kɑˈfe], *Cousin* [kuˈzɛ̃].

SECTION 2: *ch (Conclusion)*

[χ]

In Chapter 5, it was pointed out that *ch* is regularly pronounced as the voiceless velar fricative [χ] after *a, o, u,* and *au: Bach* [bɑχ], *doch* [dɔχ].

[ç]

1. After all other vowels and after consonants, *ch* is pronounced as the voiceless palatal fricative [ç]. It is especially important to be aware of this distinction in related forms with and without umlaut: *Buch* [buχ] (book), *Bücher* [ˈbyçɒ] (books); *lachen* [ˈlɑχən] (laugh), *lächerlich* [ˈlɛçɒlɪç] (ridiculous).

2. At the beginning of a few words *ch* is [ç], for example:

Cherub [ˈçerup]	(cherub)
China [ˈçinɑ]	(China)

---

[1] See Chapter 14 for *ck.*
[2] In *Cello, Cembalo, c* is [tʃ].

[k]

In a number of words of Greek origin, the spelling *ch* represents the pronunciation [k]; learn to recognize the following:

Charakter	melancholisch
Chor	Orchester
Choral	Chronik
Christ	

Exercise 15.1

Pronounce:

1. verachten, verächtlich, Buch, Bücher, durchaus
2. Loch, Löcher, hoch, höchste, Kirchhof
3. Flucht, flüchtig, Sprache, Gespräch, Fichte
4. flechten, flocht, sprechen, sprach, gesprochen
5. Gedächtnis, dachte, Geschichte, dicht, Psyche
6. missachten, Macht, mächtig, bezeichnet, Dolch
7. durchschleichen, Melancholie, Eiche, Cabaret, Cäcilie
8. Drache, christlich, chaotisch, Chor, Echo
9. Rauch, räuchern, chinesisch, mochte, möchte

Excerpts

1. Ach! denkt das Veilchen,
     Wär' ich nur die schönste Blume der Natur,
       Ach, nur ein kleines Weilchen,
       Bis mich das Liebchen abgepflückt
       Und an dem Busen matt gedrückt,
       Ach nur ein Viertelstündchen lang.
       Ach, aber ach! das Mädchen kam
       Und nicht in Acht das Veilchen nahm,
       Ertrat das arme Veilchen.

Das Veilchen
Mozart

2. Ich möchte nicht mehr leben,
     Möcht augenblicks, augenblicks verderben,
     Und möchte doch auch leben für dich, mit dir,
     Und nimmer, nimmer sterben.
     Ach, rede, sprich ein Wort nur,
     Ein einziges, ein klares. . . .

Nicht mehr zu dir zu gehen
Brahms

Tape Make a tape of the following song text:

> Wehe, Lüftchen, lind und lieblich,
> Um die Wange der Geliebten,
> Spiele zart in ihrer Locke,
> Eile nicht, hinweg zu fliehn!
> Tut sie dann vielleicht die Frage,
> Wie es um mich Armen stehe,
> Sprich: "Unendlich war sein Wehe,
> Höchst bedenklich seine Lage;
> Aber jetzo kann er hoffen,
> Wieder herrlich aufzuleben,
> Denn du, Holde, denkst an ihn."
> > *Botschaft*
> > Brahms

Songs Sing the following songs, paying special attention to the pronunciation of *ch*.

Freut euch des Lebens

D.C. al Fine

lässt das Veil - chen un - be - merkt, das uns am We - ge blüht.
sie - delt sich Zu - frie - den - heit so ger - ne bei ihm ein.
reicht die Freund - schaft schwes - ter - lich dem Red - li - chen die Hand.
wallt man froh, so wallt man leicht ins bess - re Va - ter - land.

Brüderchen, komm, tanz mit mir

1. Brü - der - chen, komm, tanz mit   mir,   bei - de Händ - chen   reich ich dir,
2. Tan - zen soll ich ar - mer Wicht?   Gre - tel, nein, das   kann ich nicht!
3. Mit dem Köpf - chen nick, nick, nick,   mit dem finger - chen   tick, tick, tick.
4. Ei, das hast du fein ge - macht,   ei, das hätt ich   nicht ge - dacht.
5. Mit den Händ - chen klapp, klapp, klapp,   mit den füss - chen   trapp, trapp, trapp.

1. ein - mal hin,   ein - mal her,   rings - her - um, das   ist nicht schwer.
2. Drum zeig mir,   wie es Brauch,   dass ich tan - zen   ler - ne auch.
3. Ein - mal hin,   ein - mal her,   rings - her - um, das   ist nicht schwer.
4. Seht mir doch   den Hansl an,   wie der Hans - l   tan - zen kann!
5. Ein - mal hin,   ein - mal her,   rings - her - um, das   ist nicht schwer.

SECTION 3: *chs*

One Element: [ks]

When *chs* occurs within one element, it is pronounced [ks]: *wachsen* ['vɑksən] (grow).

Since it can be seen from the next paragraph that a rather sizable number of forms can be derived in which *chs* is *not* pronounced [ks], the singer should become familiar with some common words containing *chs* within one element:

Achse	(axle)	Sachsen	(Saxony)
Achsel	(shoulder)	sechs	(six)
Büchse	(rifle, box)	Wachs	(wax)
Dachs	(badger)	wachsen	(grow)
Deichsel	(shaft)	du wächst	(you grow)
Drechsler	(turner)	er wächst	(he grows)
Fuchs	(fox)	er wuchs	(he grew)
Fuchsie	(fuchsia)	wechseln	(change)
Gewächs	(growth)	Weichsel	(kind of cherry)
Lachs	(salmon)	wichsen	(polish)
Luchs	(lynx)	du wichst	(you polish)
Ochse	(ox)	er wichst	(he polishes)

Two Elements

When *ch* belongs to one element and *s* to the next, each must of course be pronounced with its element, and in accordance with the rules for *ch* and *s* respectively.

1. *ch* + verb ending *-st:*
   du lachst [lɑχst] (you laugh) < lachen
   du weichst [vaeçst] (you retreat) < weichen
2. *ch* + noun ending *-s:*
   des Bachs [bɑχs] (of the brook) < Bach
   des Blechs [blɛçs] (of the metal) < Blech
3. *ch* + superlative suffix *-st:*
   höchst [høçst] (highest)
   herrlichsten ['hɛrlIçstən] (most splendid)
4. compounds:
   durchspielen ['dUrçʃpilən] (play through)
   Lochsäge ['lɔχˌzɛgə] (keyhole saw)

Exercise 15.2   Pronounce:

1. sechs, wechselt, wachsen, Fuchs, Buchs
2. erbleichst, Deichsel, Lachs, Bachs, lachst
3. wichst, sprichst, brichst, Gewächs, Gesprächs

4. Büchse, herrlichste, siegreichsten, Buchstabe
5. weichst, Weichsel, Königreichs, lieblichsten
6. huldreichstes, höchsten, nächste, wächst
7. Gebrauchs, Gefährlichsten, durchsetzen, wachsam

Exercise 15.3   Transcribe the words in Exercise 15.2 into the IPA.

Chapter 16 | The Sounds of w, v, f

SECTION 1: *w*

[v]

The letter *w* is almost always pronounced [v]: *Wein* [vɑen] (wine), *zwei* [tsvɑe] (two).

Exercise 16.1   Pronounce:

1. woher, gewohnt, entzwei, zwanzig, zwölf
2. schwarz, schwingen, wegwerfen, Löwe, wogten
3. Juwel, jeweils, Möwe, bewegt, beschwört

Excerpts

1. Jeder wird sich glücklich scheinen,
   Wenn mein Bild vor ihm erscheint;
   Eine Träne wird er weinen,
   Und ich weiss nicht, was er weint.

   Harfenspieler
   Wolf

2. O wer sehen könnte, welche Bilder
   Hinter dieser Stirne, diesen schwarzen
   Wimpern sich in sanftem Wechsel malen!

   Schlafendes Jesuskind
   Wolf

3. Ach, es entschwindet mit tauigem Flügel
   Mir auf den wiegenden Wellen die Zeit.
   Morgen entschwinde mit schimmerndem Flügel
   Wieder wie gestern und heute die Zeit,
   Bis ich auf höherem strahlendem Flügel
   Selber entschwinde der wechselnden Zeit.

   Lied auf dem Wasser zu singen
   Schubert

Song   Sing the following song, concentrating on the pronunciation of *w* (note that *v* is usually pronounced [f]).

Morgen will mein Schatz verreisen

Mor - gen will mein Schatz ver - rei - sen,   Ab - schied neh - men mit Ge -
Sa - ssen da zwei Tur - tel - tau - ben,   sa - ssen wohl auf grü - nem
Laub und Gras, das mag ver - wel - ken,   a - ber uns - re Lie - be
Ei - ne Schwal - be macht kein'n Som - mer,   ob sie gleich die er - ste

walt.   Drau - ssen sin - gen schon die Vö - gel,   sin - gen schon die
Ast.   Wo sich zwei ver - lieb - te schei - den,   zwei ver - lieb - te
nicht.   Du kommst mir aus mei - nen Au - gen,   mir aus mei - nen
ist;   und mein Lieb - chen macht mir Kum - mer,   Lieb - chen macht mir

Vö - gel in dem grü - nen, grü - nen Wald.
schei - den, da ver - wel - ken Laub und Gras.
Au - gen, a - ber aus dem Her - zen nicht.
Kum - mer, ob sie gleich die Schön - ste ist.   Denn es fällt mir so schwer aus der

Hei - mat zu gehn, wenn die Hoff - nung nicht wär auf ein

Wie - der, Wie - der-sehn, le - be wohl, le - be wohl, le - be

wohl, le - be wohl, le - be wohl, auf Wie - der___ sehn!

SECTION 2: *v*

[f]

In words of Germanic origin, *v* is pronounced [f]: *viel* [fil] (much), *Bevölkerung*
[bə'fœlkərUŋ] (population). It is also pronounced [f] in

Vers [fɛrs] (verse)
Veilchen ['faelçən] (violet)
Vogt [fokt] (warden, governor)

[v]

In most words of foreign origin, *v* is pronounced [v] before a vowel: *Vase* ['vazə], *Klavier* [klaˈvir], *braver* ['brɑvɒ]. However, like *b, d, g, s,* it becomes unvoiced in final position or before a consonant: *brav* [brɑf], *bravster* ['brɑfstɒ].

Exercise 16.2   Pronounce:

1. Vater, völlig, vervollständigen, Violine, vom
2. brave, brav, nervös, Nerv, Villa, Venus
3. Klavier, Frevel, Frevler, Provinz, November
4. Vetter, Novelle, Viola, vielleicht, Sklave
5. bevor, davon, Virtuose, Veilchen, Vers, verweht
6. Levkoje, Tonverschiebung, Pulver, privat, Universität

Excerpt

So wandelt froh auf Gottes Wegen,
Und was ihr thut, das thut getreu!
Verdienet eures Gottes Segen,
Denn der ist alle Morgen neu:
Denn welcher seine Zuversicht
Auf Gott setzt, den verlässt er nicht.

Wer nur den lieben Gott lässt walten
Bach

Song   Sing the following song, concentrating on the pronunciation of *v*.

Wieder einmal ausgeflogen

Wie - der ein - mal aus - ge - flo - gen, wie - der ein - mal heim - ge -
Wird uns wie - der wohl ver - ei - nen, fri - scher Ost und fri - scher
Im - mer schwe - rer wird das Päck - chen, kaum noch trägt es sich al -
Und an sei - nes Hau - ses Schwel - le wird ein je - der fest ge -

kehrt, fand ich doch die al - ten Freun - de, fand ich
West? Auch die lo - se - sten der Vö - gel, auch die
lein, und in im - mer eng - re Fes - seln, und in
bannt, a - ber Lie - bes - fä - den spin - nen, a - ber

doch die al - ten Freun - de und die Her - zen un - ver - sehrt.
lo - se - sten der Vö - gel tra - gen all - ge - mach zu Nest.
im - mer eng - re Fes - seln schlin - get uns die Hei - mat ein.
Lie - bes - fä - den spin - nen heim - lich sich von Land zu Land.

SECTION 3: *f*

[f]

The letter *f* is always pronounced [f]: *fein* [fɑen] (fine), *Brief* [brif] (letter), *gefragt* [gə'frɑkt] (asked).

ff

[f]

When *ff* occurs within one element, it is pronounced [f]: *treffen* ['trɛfən] (meet), *trifft* [trɪft] (meets).

[ff]

Occasionally, *ff* constitutes parts of two elements, in which case the sound is prolonged: *auffahren* ['ɑofˌfɑrən] (rise).

Exercise 16.3

Pronounce:

1. Fuge, fällen, führen, Efeu, rufen
2. Neffe, Ofen, offen, Öfen, öffnen
3. schlafe, schlaffe, aufliegen, auffliegen, auffallen
4. Stiefvater, aufragen, befragen, schroff, pfiff
5. Pfeife, Haufen, häufig, schafft, Schaft, verblüfft

Tape

Make a tape of the following song text:

Wie Melodien zieht es mir leise durch den Sinn,
Wie Frühlingsblumen blüht es, und schwebt wie Duft dahin.
Doch kommt das Wort und fasst es und führt es vor das Aug',
Wie Nebelgrau erblasst es und schwindet wie ein Hauch.
Und dennoch ruht im Reime verborgen wohl ein Duft,
Den mild aus stillem Keime ein feuchtes Auge ruft.

Wie Melodien Zieht es mir
Brahms

Chapter 17 | The Sounds of m, n

SECTION 1: *m*

[m]

The letter *m* is pronounced [m] as in English: *mein* [mɑen] (my), *kamen* ['kɑmən] (came).

mm

[m]

Normally, *mm* belongs to one element and is pronounced [m]: *Flamme* ['flɑmə] (flame), *flammt* [flɑmt] (flames).

[mm]

In a few instances, *mm* represents parts of two elements and the pronunciation is extended: *ummalen* ['Um͵mɑlen] (repaint). Since many coaches recommend beginning the articulation of *m* on one note and concluding it on the next, there is little effective difference in singing between [m] and [mm]. The same applies to *n* and *nn*.

Excerpt

Mach' auf, mach' auf, doch leise, mein Kind,
Um Keinen vom Schlummer zu wecken;
Kaum murmelt der Bach, kaum zittert im Wind
Ein Blatt an den Büschen und Hecken.
Drum leise, mein Mädchen, dass nichts sich regt,
Nur leise die Hand auf die Klinke gelegt.

Ständchen
Strauss

SECTION 2: *n*

[n]

As in English, *n* is pronounced [n]: *nein* [naen] (no), *blind* [blInt] (blind).

nn

[n]

Usually, *nn* belongs to one element and is pronounced [n]: *Tanne* ['tanə] (fir), *nennt* [nɛnt] (calls).

[nn]

Since several prefixes end in *n*, *nn* sometimes represents parts of two elements: *annehmen* ['an͵nemən] (assume), *hinnehmen* ['hIn͵nemən] (accept). Although *nn* is properly transcribed [nn] in these cases, there may be little difference in pronunciation between [n] and [nn], depending on style (see *mm* above).

ng

[ŋ]

When *ng* occurs within one element it is always pronounced [ŋ]: *Finger* ['fIŋɒ], *Hunger* ['hUŋɒ], *Klang* [klaŋ] (sound).

[ng]

When *n* and *g* represent parts of two elements, they are pronounced as [n] + [g]: *angehen* ['an͵geən] (concern), *hingehen* ['hIn͵geən] (go there).

nk

[ŋk]

When *nk* occurs within one element it is always pronounced [ŋk]: *dunkel* ['dUŋkəl] (dark), *Dank* [daŋk] (thanks).

[nk]

When *n* and *k* belong to different elements, they are pronounced as [n] + [k]: *ankommen* ['an͵kɔmən] (arrive), *unklar* ['Un͵klaɾ] (unclear).

Exercise 17.1 Pronounce:

1. Ring, Doppelgänger, Meistersänger, danken, denken
2. Hingabe, hing, hingehören, hinken, hinkommen
3. angelehnt, Engel, dringlich, grimmig, kommen
4. jüngrem, Haingesträuch, Frühlingsabendrot, ringsum
5. Engelszungen, Angebinde, Tränenahnung, hinnen, herannahen
6. Mondscheinnacht, kennen, ungeleitet, unnütz, Brunnen
7. Junggeselle, Gesangstunde, Gemeingut, Jammer
8. annehmen, dennoch, angenommen, Funktion, Spengler
9. Götterfunken, klangreich, klingen, Tonkunst, Junker-Unkraut
10. Drangsal, empfangen, englisch, entlanggehen, Unglück

Exercise 17.2 Read the following transcription:

[deɒ tot dɑs ʔIst di 'kylə nɑχt
dɑs 'lebən ʔIst deɒ 'ʃvylə tɑk
ɛs 'dUŋkəlt ʃon mIç 'ʃlɛfɒt
deɒ tɑk hɑt mIç myt gə'mɑχt
'ybɒ mɑen bɛt ɛɒ'hept zIç ɑen bɑom
dɾIn zIŋt di 'jUŋə 'nɑχtigɑl
zi zIŋt fɒn 'lɑotɒ 'libə
Iç høɾ ʔɛs zo'gɑɾ ʔIm trɑom]

Excerpts

1. Wie im Morgenglanze du rings mich anglühst,
   Frühling, Geliebter!

   Ganymed
   Schubert

2. Dein Angesicht, so lieb und schön,
   Das hab' ich jüngst im Traum gesehn,
   Es ist so mild und engelgleich,
   Und doch so bleich, so schmerzenreich.

   Dein Angesicht
   Schumann

Tape Make a tape of the following song text:

1. Holder klingt der Vogelsang, wenn die Engelreine,
   Die mein Jünglingsherz bezwang, wandelt durch die Haine.
   Röter blühen Tal und Au, grüner wird der Wasen,
   Wo die Finger meiner Frau Maienblumen lasen.
   Ohne sie ist alles tot, welk sind Blüt' und Kräuter:
   Und kein Frühlingsabendrot dünkt mir schön und heiter.
   Traute, minnigliche Frau wollest nimmer fliehen,
   Dass mein Herz, gleich dieser Au,
   Mög' in Wonne Blühen, mög' in Wonne blühen.

   Minnelied
   Brahms

Songs Sing the following songs, concentrating on the sounds of *m* and *n*.

Ade, zur guten Nacht

Win - ter schneit's den Schnee: da komm ich wie - der.
mich zum Lie - ben ge-bracht mit gro - ssem Ver - lan - gen.
Herz bei Her - zen lag, das hast ver - ges - sen.
ist der Schluss ge - macht, dass ich muss schei - den.

O Tannenbaum

O Tan - nen - baum, o Tan - nen - baum, wie treu sind dei - ne
O Tan - nen - baum, o Tan - nen - baum, du kannst mir sehr ge -
O Tan - nen - baum, o Tan - nen - baum, dein Kleid will mich was

Blät - ter! Du grünst nicht nur zur Som - mers - zeit nein
fal - len. Wie oft hat nicht zur Weih - nachts - zeit ein
leh - ren. Die Hoff - nung und Be - stän - dig - keit gibt

auch im Win - ter, wenn es schneit. O Tan - nen - baum, o
Baum von dir mich hoch er - freut. O Tan - nen - baum, o
Trost und Kraft zu je - der Zeit. O Tan - nen - baum, o

Tan - nen - baum, wie treu sind dei - ne Blät - ter!
Tan - nen - baum, du kannst mir sehr ge - fal - len.
Tan - nen - baum, dein Kleid will mich was leh - ren.

Appendix A | Charts

Chart 1. English Consonants

	Bilabial	Labiodental	Dental	Alveolar	Prepalatal	Palatal	Velar	Glottal
Stops								
voiced	[b]			[d]			[g]	
voiceless	[p]			[t]			[k]	
Fricatives								
voiced		[v]	[ð]	[z]	[ʒ]			
voiceless		[f]	[θ]	[s]	[ʃ]			[h]
Affricates								
voiced					[dʒ]			
voiceless					[tʃ]			
Nasals								
voiced	[m]			[n]			[ŋ]	
Laterals								
voiced				[l]				
Trills								
voiced				[r]				
Retroflex								
voiced				[r]				
Glides								
voiced	[w]					[j]		

Chart 2. German Consonants

	Bilabial	Labiodental	Dental	Alveolar	Prepalatal	Palatal	Velar	Glottal
Stops								
voiced	[b]			[d]			[g]	
voiceless	[p]			[t]			[k]	[ʔ]
Fricatives								
voiced		[v]		[z]	[ʒ]			
voiceless		[f]		[s]	[ʃ]	[ç]	[χ]	[h]
Affricates								
voiced								
voiceless		[pf]		[ts]	[tʃ]			
Nasals								
voiced	[m]			[n]			[ŋ]	
Laterals								
voiced				[l]				
Trills								
voiced				[ɾ]				
Glides								
voiced						[j]		

Chart 3. English Vowels

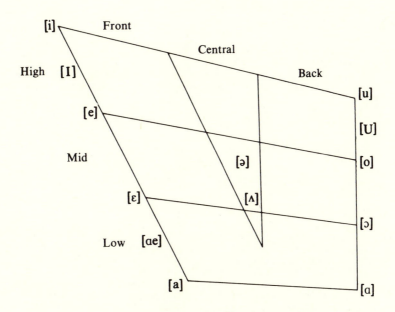

Chart 4. German Vowels

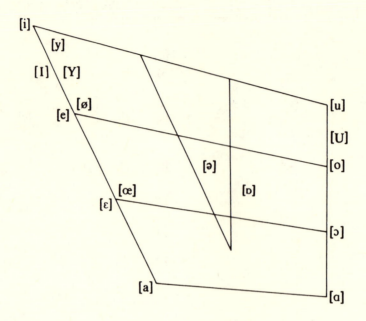

Appendix B | Additional Song Texts

Brahms   *Vergebliches Ständchen*

Guten Abend, mein Schatz,
Guten Abend, mein kind!
Ich komm' aus Lieb' zu dir,
Ach, mach' mir auf die Tür!
Mach' mir auf die Tür!

"Meine Tür ist verschlossen,
Ich lass dich nicht ein;
Mutter die rät' mir klug,
Wärst du herein mit Fug,
Wär's mit mir vorbei!"

So kalt ist die Nacht,
So eisig der Wind,
Dass mir das Herz erfriert,
Mein' Lieb' erlöschen wird;
Öffne mir, mein Kind!

"Löschet dein Lieb'
Lass sie löschen nur!
Löschet sie immer zu,
Geh' heim zu Bett zur Ruh',
Gute Nacht, mein Knab'!"

Schubert   *An die Musik*

Du holde Kunst, in wieviel grauen Stunden,
Wo mich des Lebens wilder Kreis umstrickt,
Hast du mein Herz zu warmer Lieb' entzunden,
Hast mich in eine bessre Welt entrückt!

Oft hat ein Seufzer, deiner Harf' entflossen,
Ein süsser, heiliger Akkord von dir,
Den Himmel bessrer Zeiten mir erschlossen,
Du holde Kunst, ich danke dir dafür!

Du bist die Ruh'

Du bist die Ruh',
Der Friede mild,
Die Sehnsucht du,
Und was sie stillt.

Ich weihe dir
Voll Lust und Schmerz
Zur Wohnung hier
Mein Aug' und Herz.

Kehr ein bei mir
Und schliesse du
Still hinter dir
Die Pforten zu!

Treib andern Schmerz
Aus dieser Brust!
Voll sei dies Herz
Von deiner Lust.

Dies Augenzelt
Von deinem Glanz
Allein erhellt,
O füll es ganz!

Erlkönig

Wer reitet so spät durch Nacht und Wind?
Es ist der Vater mit seinem Kind;
Er hat den Knaben wohl in dem Arm,
Er fasst ihn sicher, er hält ihn warm.

Mein Sohn, was birgst du so bang dein Gesicht?—
Siehst, Vater, du den Erlkönig nicht?
Den Erlenkönig mit Kron' und Schweif?—
Mein Sohn, es ist ein Nebelstreif.—

"Du liebes Kind, komm, geh mit mir!
Gar schöne Spiele spiel' ich mit dir,
Manch bunte Blumen sind an dem Strand,
Meine Mutter hat manch gülden Gewand."

Mein Vater, mein Vater, und hörest du nicht,
Was Erlenkönig mir leise verspricht?—
Sei ruhig, bleibe ruhig, mein Kind:
In dürren Blättern säuselt der Wind.—

"Willst, feiner Knabe, du mit mir gehn?
Meine Töchter sollen dich warten schön;
Meine Töchter führen den nächtlichen Reihn
Und wiegen und tanzen und singen dich ein."

Mein Vater, mein Vater, und siehst du nicht dort
Erlkönigs Töchter am düstern Ort?—
Mein Sohn, mein Sohn, ich seh' es genau:
Es scheinen die alten Weiden so grau.—

"Ich liebe dich, mich reizt deine schöne Gestalt;
Und bist du nicht willig, so brauch' ich Gewalt."
Mein Vater, mein Vater, jetzt fasst er mich an!
Erlkönig hat mir ein Leids getan!—

Dem Vater grauset's, er reitet geschwind,
Er hält in Armen das ächzende Kind,
Erreicht den Hof mit Mühe und Not;
In seinen Armen das Kind war tot.

Die Forelle

In einem Bächlein helle,
Da schoss in froher Eil'
Die launige Forelle
Vorüber wie ein Pfeil.
Ich stand an dem Gestade,
Und sah in süsser Ruh'
Des muntern Fisches Bade
Im klaren Bächlein zu.

Ein Fischer mit der Rute
Wohl an dem Ufer stand,
Und sah's mit kaltem Blute,
Wie sich das Fischlein wand.
So lang dem Wasser helle,
So dacht' ich, nicht gebricht,
So fängt er die Forelle
Mit seiner Angel nicht.

Doch plötzlich ward dem Diebe
Die Zeit zu lang. Er macht
Das Bächlein tückisch trübe,
Und eh' ich es gedacht;—
So zuckte seine Rute,
Das Fischlein zappelt dran,
Und ich mit regem Blute
Sah die Betrogne an.

Gretchen am Spinnrade

Meine Ruh ist hin,
Mein Herz ist schwer;
Ich finde sie nimmer
Und nimmermehr.

Wo ich ihn nicht hab'
Ist mir das Grab,
Die ganze Welt
Ist mir vergällt.

Mein armer Kopf
Ist mir verrückt,
Mein armer Sinn
Ist mir zerstückt.

Meine Ruh ist hin,
Mein Herz ist schwer;
Ich finde sie nimmer
Und nimmermehr.

Nach ihm nur schau' ich
Zum Fenster hinaus,
Nach ihm nur geh' ich
Aus dem Haus.

Sein hoher Gang,
Sein' edle Gestalt,
Seines Mundes Lächeln,
Seiner Augen Gewalt,

Und seiner Rede
Zauberfluss,
Sein Händedruck,
Und ach, sein Kuss!

Meine Ruh ist hin,
Mein Herz ist schwer;
Ich finde sie nimmer
Und nimmermehr.

Mein Busen drängt
Sich nach ihm hin;
Ach, dürft' ich fassen
Und halten ihn

Und küssen ihn,
So wie ich wollt',
An seinen Küssen
Vergehen sollt'!

Die junge Nonne

Wie braust durch die Wipfel der heulende Sturm!
Es klirren die Balken, es zittert das Haus!
Es rollet der Donner, es leuchtet der Blitz,
Und finster die Nacht wie das Grab!

Immerhin, immerhin,
So tobt' es auch jüngst noch in mir!
Es brauste das Leben, wie jetzo der Sturm,
Es bebten die Glieder, wie jetzo das Haus,
Es flammte die Liebe, wie jetzo der Blitz,
Und finster die Brust wie das Grab!

Nun tobe, du wilder, gewalt'ger Sturm,
Im Herzen ist Friede, im Herzen ist Ruh,
Des Bräutigams harret die liebende Braut,
Gereinigt in prüfender Glut,
Der ewigen Liebe getraut.

Ich harre, mein Heiland, mit sehnendem Blick!
Komm, himmlischer Bräutigam, hole die Braut,
Erlöse die Seele von irdischer Haft!
Horch, friedlich ertönet das Glöcklein vom Turm!
Es lockt mir das süsse Getön
Allmächtig zu ewigen Höhn.
Alleluja!

Der Tod und das Mädchen

DAS MÄDCHEN
Vorüber, ach vorüber
Geh, wilder Knochenmann!
Ich bin noch jung! Geh, Lieber,
Und rühre mich nicht an!

DER TOD
Gib deine Hand, du schön und zart Gebild!
Bin Freund und komme nicht zu strafen.
Sei gutes Muts! Ich bin nicht wild!
Sollst sanft in meinen Armen schlafen!

Wohin?

Ich hört' ein Bächlein rauschen
Wohl aus dem Felsenquell,
Hinab zum Tale rauschen
So frisch und wunderhell.

Ich weiss nicht, wie mir wurde,
Nicht, wer den Rat mir gab,
Ich musste gleich hinunter
Mit meinem Wanderstab.

Hinunter und immer weiter,
Und immer dem Bache nach,
Und immer frischer rauschte,
Und immer heller der Bach.

Ist das denn meine Strasse?
O Bächlein, sprich, wohin?
Du hast mit deinem Rauschen
Mir ganz berauscht den Sinn.

Was sag' ich denn von Rauschen?
Das kann kein Rauschen sein!
Es singen wohl die Nixen
Dort unten ihren Reihn.

Lass singen, Gesell, lass rauschen,
Und wandre fröhlich nach!
Es gehn ja Mühlenräder
In jedem klaren Bach.

Schumann   *Du bist wie eine Blume*

Du bist wie eine Blume
So hold und schön und rein;
Ich schau' dich an, und Wehmut
Schleicht mir ins Herz hinein.

Mir ist, als ob ich die Hände
Aufs Haupt dir legen sollt'
Betend, dass Gott dich erhalte
So rein und schön und hold.

Du Ring an meinem Finger

Du Ring an meinem Finger,
Mein goldenes Ringelein,
Ich drücke dich fromm an die Lippen,
Dich fromm an das Herze mein.

Ich hatt' ihn ausgeträumet,
Der Kindheit friedlichen Traum,
Ich fand allein mich verloren
Im öden, unendlichen Raum.

Du Ring an meinem Finger,
Da hast du mich erst belehrt,
Hast meinem Blick erschlossen
Des Lebens unendlichen Wert.

Ich werd' ihm dienen, ihm leben,
Ihm angehören ganz,
Hin selber mich geben und finden
Verklärt mich in seinem Glanz.

Du Ring an meinem Finger,
Mein goldenes Ringelein,
Ich drücke dich fromm an die Lippen,
Dich fromm an das Herze mein.

Frühlingsnacht

Übern Garten durch die Lüfte
Hört ich Wandervögel ziehn,
Das bedeutet Frühlingsdüfte,
Unten fängts schon an zu blühn.

Jauchzen möcht ich, möchte weinen,
Ist mirs doch, als könnts nicht sein,
Alte Wunder wieder scheinen
Mit dem Mondesglanz herein.

Und der Mond, die Sterne sagen's,
Und in Träumen rauscht's der Hain,
Und die Nachtigallen schlagen's:
Sie ist deine, sie ist dein!

Ich grolle nicht

Ich grolle nicht, und wenn das Herz auch bricht,
Ewig verlornes Lieb! ich grolle nicht.
Wie du auch strahlst in Diamantenpracht,
Es fällt kein Strahl in deines Herzensnacht.

Das weiss ich längst. Ich sah dich ja im Traum,
Und sah die Nacht in deines Herzens Raum,
Und sah die Schlang', die dir am Herzen frisst,
Ich sah, mein Lieb, wie sehr du elend bist.

Die Lotosblume

Die Lotosblume ängstigt
Sich vor der Sonne Pracht,
Und mit gesenktem Haupte
Erwartet sie träumend die Nacht.

Der Mond, der ist ihr Buhle,
Er weckt sie mit seinem Licht,
Und ihm entschleiert sie freundlich
Ihr frommes Blumengesicht.

Sie blüht und glüht und leuchtet
Und starret stumm in die Höh';
Sie duftet und weinet und zittert
Vor Liebe und Liebesweh.

Mondnacht

Es war, als hätt der Himmel
Die Erde still geküsst,
Dass sie im Blütenschimmer
Von ihm nun träumen müsst.

Die Luft ging durch die Felder,
Die Ähren wogten sacht,
Es rauschten leis die Wälder,
So sternklar war die Nacht.

Und meine Seele spannte
Weit ihre Flügel aus,
Flog durch die stillen Lande,
Als flöge sie nach Haus.

Strauss   *Traum durch die Dämmerung*

Weite Wiesen im Dämmergrau;
Die Sonne verglomm, die Sterne ziehn;
Nun geh ich zu der schönsten Frau,
Weit über Wiesen im Dämmergrau,
Tief in den Busch von Jasmin.

Durch Dämmergrau in der Liebe Land;
Ich gehe nicht schnell, ich eile nicht;
Mich zieht ein weiches, samtenes Band
Durch Dämmergrau in der Liebe Land,
In ein blaues, mildes Licht.

Morgen

Und Morgen wird die Sonne wieder scheinen,
Und auf dem Wege, den ich gehen werde,
Wird uns, die Seligen, sie wieder einen,
Inmitten dieser sonnenatmenden Erde . . .

Und zu dem Strand, dem weiten, wogenblauen,
Werden wir still und langsam niedersteigen.
Stumm werden wir uns in die Augen schauen,
Und auf uns sinkt des Glückes grosses Schweigen.

Wolf *Anakreons Grab*

Wo die Rose hier blüht, wo Reben um Lorbeer sich schlingen,
Wo das Turtelchen lockt, wo sich das Grillchen ergötzt,
Welch ein Grab ist hier, das alle Götter mit Leben
Schön bepflanzt und geziert? Es ist Anakreons Ruh.
Frühling, Sommer und Herbst genoss der glückliche Dichter;
Vor dem Winter hat ihn endlich der Hügel geschützt.

Er ist's

Frühling lässt sein blaues Band
Wieder flattern durch die Lüfte;
Süsse, wohlbekannte Düfte
Streifen ahnungsvoll das Land.
Veilchen träumen schon,
Wollen balde kommen.
—Horch, von fern ein leiser Harfenton!
Frühling, ja du bist's!
Dich hab' ich vernommen!

Mignon—1

Kennst du das Land, wo die Zitronen blühn,
Im dunkeln Laub die Gold-Orangen glühn,
Ein sanfter Wind vom blauen Himmel weht,
Die Myrte still und hoch der Lorbeer steht?
Kennst du es wohl?—Dahin! Dahin!
Möcht' ich mit dir, o mein Geliebter, ziehn.

Kennst du das Haus? Auf Säulen ruht sein Dach,
Es glänzt der Saal, es schimmert das Gemach,
Und Mormorbilder stehn und sehn mich an:

Was hat man dir, du armes Kind, getan?
Kennst du es wohl?—Dahin! Dahin!
Möcht' ich mit dir, o mein Beschützer, ziehn.

Kennst du den Berg und seinen Wolkensteg?
Das Maultier sucht im Nebel seinen Weg;
In Höhlen wohnt der Drachen alte Brut;
Es stürzt der Fels und über ihn die Flut.
Kennst du ihn wohl?—Dahin! Dahin
Geht unser Weg; o Vater, lass uns ziehn!

Mignon—3

Nur wer die Sehnsucht kennt,
Weiss, was ich leide!
Allein und abgetrennt
Von aller Freude
Seh' ich ans Firmament
Nach jener Seite.
Ach! der mich liebt und kennt,
Ist in der Weite.
Es schwindelt mir, es brennt
Mein Eingeweide.
Nur wer die Sehnsucht kennt
Weiss was ich leide!

Verborgenheit

Lass, o Welt, o lass mich sein!
Locket nicht mit Liebesgaben,
Lasst dies Herz alleine haben
Seine Wonne, seine Pein!

Was ich traure, weiss ich nicht,
Es ist unbekanntes Wehe;
Immerdar durch Tränen sehe
Ich der Sonne liebes Licht.

Oft bin ich mir kaum bewusst,
Und die helle Freude zücket
Durch die Schwere, die mich drücket,
Wonniglich in meiner Brust.

Lass, o Welt, o lass mich sein!
Locket nicht mit Liebesgaben,
Lasst dies Herz alleine haben
Seine Wonne, seine Pein!

Das verlassene Mägdlein

Früh, wann die Hähne krähn,
Eh' die Sternlein verschwinden,
Muss ich am Herde stehn,
Muss Feuer zünden.

Schön ist der Flammen Schein,
Es springen die Funken;
Ich schaue so drein,
In Leid versunken.

Plötzlich, da kommt es mir,
Treuloser Knabe,
Dass ich die Nacht von dir
Geträumet habe.

Träne auf Träne dann
Stürzet hernieder;
So kommt der Tag heran—
O ging' er wieder!